LET THE ADVERTISING AGENTS TAKE CHARGE OF THE BARTHOLDI BUSINESS,
AND THE MONEY WILL BE RAISED WITHOUT DELAY.

The Art of Ill Will

The Art of Ill Will

The Story of American Political Cartoons

Donald Dewey

New York University Press

NEW YORK AND LONDON

NEW YORK UNIVERSITY PRESS
New York and London
www.nyupress.org

Unless otherwise credited, all cartoons are from
The Granger Collection, New York; www.granger.com

Library of Congress Cataloging-in-Publication Data
Dewey, Donald, 1940–
The art of ill will : the story of American political cartoons /
Donald Dewey.
p.   cm.
Includes bibliographical references and index.
ISBN-13: 978-0-8147-1985-5 (alk. paper)
ISBN-10: 0-8147-1985-6 (alk. paper)
1. American wit and humor, Pictorial—History.   2. United States—
Politics and government—Caricatures and cartoons.   I. Title.
NC1420.D49   2007
741.5′358—dc22   2007001909

Book design by Charles B. Hames. Book composition by Andrew Katz.

New York University Press books are printed on acid-free paper,
and their binding materials are chosen for strength and durability.

Printed and bound in China

10 9 8 7 6 5 4 3 2 1

For William Glover and Lila Dlaboha

For their inspiration and encouragement and, not least,
for making available the vast resources of The Granger
Collection, the eminent historical picture library
in New York that supplied the overwhelming
majority of the artwork in this book.

Outside of basic intelligence, there is
nothing more important to a
good political cartoonist
than ill will.

—Jules Feiffer

The political cartoon has always served
as a special prod—a reminder to
public servants that they
are public servants.

—Herbert Block (Herblock)

Contents

Introduction

The Story of American Political Cartoons

1. Politics

Editorial cartoons honed their political blades on the technologies, opportunities, and pressures of the nineteenth-century mass media. Had nothing of the kind existed before? Of course it had. Wherever there had been a cave wall and a sharp-edged rock or a city wall and a piece of coal, political wits can be presumed to have declared a conviction masked as drollery. In their book *The Ungentlemanly Art*, Stephen Hess and Milton Kaplan mark the claim for the oldest extant cartoon as dating back to around 1360 B.C.E.; the target was Akhenaten (Amenhotep IV), the pharaoh husband of Queen Nofretete, who had alienated Egyptians by imposing monotheism on his kingdom.[1] In ancient Greece, Aristotle was said to have railed against the grotesqueries that foreshadowed cartoon caricatures; in classical Rome, frescoes executed at Pompeii and Herculaneum betrayed less than a reverent spirit toward their subjects. Other conspicuous examples of pictorial political statements came from Renaissance Italy, sixteenth-century Reformation Germany, and the eighteenth-century London of William Hogarth. Jonathan Swift, for one, could not get enough of Hogarth's graphic commentaries on such debacles as the stock market collapse of 1720. In one poem, Swift implored the artist to "draw them so that we may trace / all the soul in every face."[2] Such masters as Lucas Cranach the Elder and Hans Holbein the Younger in Germany and Francisco Goya in Spain have ties to the art form. Somewhat further afield, but noteworthy because of his melding of political and aesthetic convictions during the French Revolution, was Jacques-Louis David.

But there are limits to citing such precedents. Intriguing as they might be, for example, the contentions about the Akhenaten illustration resemble the enchanted history that has claimed the sands around the pyramids as the first primitive baseball diamond and Babylonians as the first vaudeville comics: research dreaming after relevance. Critic Isabel Simeral Johnson also noted that one of the familiar features of an effective political cartoon—caricature—probably wasn't even present in the depiction of the pharaoh. "[His] features were so abnormally ugly that it is difficult to tell a caricature of him from an authentic portrait," Johnson observed.[3] She had a point since Akhenaten always insisted that the artists he surrounded himself with render him naturally; in his case, that meant an egg-shaped head, a horsey jaw, a thick neck, weak, gangly arms, and a well-tended paunch. The most malicious of Egyptian

caricaturists would have been hard pressed to offer something creepier than the original.[4]

In the United States, there is little argument that the earliest example of political cartoon art of any kind involved that most fertile of colonial minds, Benjamin Franklin's. Beyond that, there is some debate. The work with the widest claim to having been first was published on May 9, 1754. In preparation for an Albany conference for discussing relations with the Iroquois, Franklin wrote an editorial in the Pennsylvania *Gazette* bemoaning a lack of unity among the colonies on the question and warning of Iroquois attacks within the context of looming hostilities between England and France. The editorial was accompanied by a woodcut drawing entitled "Join, or Die," which pictured an undulating snake divided into eight pieces (the number of colonial governments). The snake symbol touched on a superstition at the time that a serpent cut in two would come to life again if its pieces were rejoined before sundown. The combination of alarmism and appeal to community

spirit spurred the Albany Congress into passing an elaborate unification plan, and the woodcut was reproduced by numerous journals in New York, Boston, and other centers up and down the east coast. (Preferring to accent the positive, the Boston *Gazette* recaptioned it "Unite and Conquer.") Moreover, in slightly modified form, it was recirculated in subsequent years as a rallying point for the colonists in their struggles against the British. All that was the good news. The bad news was that the unification plan presented by Franklin in Albany was subsequently spurned by both the legislatures of the separate colonies and England, and for the same reason—they didn't want to cede power to any supracolonial body. Thus, if "Join, or Die" was not definitely the first American political cartoon, it was certainly the first to have its politics rejected.

The principal rival to the "Join, or Die" claim to primacy was also a Franklin creation, a much more crudely produced 1746 piece entitled *Non Votis* or "The Waggoner and Hercules." Drawn eight years before "Join, or Die" to illustrate the pamphlet *Plain Truth*, the work depicts a driver praying that Hercules come down from his heavenly cloud to pull the man's wagon out of mud. The intended moral was a Franklin favorite: God helps those who help themselves. In this particular instance, he was trying to whip up Pennsylvanians to protect their land from threatening Indians, even if doing so entailed defending Quakers who declined to protect themselves. He later asserted that the pamphlet and the cartoon were decisive for raising a militia of some ten thousand volunteers. If *Non Votis* has not won as much recognition as "Join, or Die" as the start of American political cartooning, it is largely because the parable being illustrated had been around since Aesop and, unlike the lettering in the snake drawing, had no explicit references to the issue under debate in the colonies.

As the subject rather than the designer, Franklin additionally figured in seminal copper-plate images produced in Pennsylvania between 1764 and 1765. Here again, his attitude toward Native Americans was front and center, this time as a double-dealer who publicly condemned the massacre of a peaceful Conestoga village by a band of cutthroats, but who also prevented vengeance-bent citizens from going after the killers. One of the plates portrayed Franklin as an agent of the devil for stemming the retribution. The artwork helped cost him his seat in Pennsylvania Assembly elections held shortly afterward, arguably making for the first instance of graphic work influencing local politics.[5]

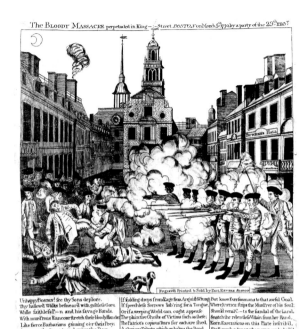

As charged as it was in its meaning and as familiar as it became to the colonists, "Join, or Die" didn't spark any mass rush to wood blocks. In the decades that followed the original publication of the Franklin design, the genre's most discussed figure was the "Join, or Die" engraver, Paul Revere, and not because he was galloping through the night warning about the British coming; he wouldn't even admit to sharing the objectives of political cartoonists. Revere was a silversmith by profession—a capricious trade economically that often forced him to moonlight as an engraver for extra income. One of his pieces ("The Bloody Massacre") purported to depict the March 5, 1770, Boston Massacre, when British soldiers fired into a hectoring crowd of colonists, killing three of them on the spot and wounding two others fatally.

Revere's engraving of a wanton slaughter (hand-colored for greater effect) came under attack on a couple of fronts—as anti-British propaganda passing itself off as reporting and as theft (of the work of artist Henry Pelham) passing itself off as original work. The midnight rider made legend by Henry Wadsworth Longfellow's *Tales of a Wayside Inn* was untroubled, turning out yet other pictures on the same theme, including one that identified five coffins as those of the colonists killed in the shooting. The engravings were regarded as so inflammatory that future president John Adams, one of the lawyers for the British soldiers accused of the blood-bath, sought a change of venue for a trial. The defense didn't succeed in that goal, but it did manage to win acquittals for seven of the nine Britons charged, including the commanding officer.[6]

The climate was only slightly less contentious around the publication of "The Federal Superstructure," a product of the often-bitter wrangling over articles of the Constitution. Published by the Massachusetts *Centinel* on January 30, 1788, the pro-Constitution drawing showed a hand raising a pillar identified as Massachusetts to an upright position so that it would be aligned with the pillars of Delaware, Pennsylvania, Connecticut, New Jersey, and Georgia (states that had already ratified the charter). In case the meaning wasn't clear enough, the *Centinel* (which ran the series through August) captioned the work as "The Pillar of the Great Federal Edifice rises daily."

Hearsay dates the first American cartoon mockery of a president to the days around the inauguration of George Washington in May 1789. In a letter to Horatio Gates, a fellow general from the War of Independence, John

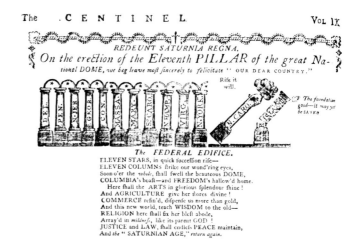

Armstrong reported from the inauguration scene in New York City that "all the world here are busy in collecting flowers and sweets of every kind to amuse and delight the President. . . . Yet in the midst of this admiration there are skeptics who doubt its propriety, and wits who amuse themselves at its extravagance. . . . A caricature has already appeared, called 'The Entry,' full of very disloyal and profane allusions."[7] Although no copy of "The Entry" survives, it reputedly showed Washington being led on a donkey by one of his aides, David Humphreys. A couplet told readers that "the glorious time has come to pass / When David shall conduct an ass."[8]

For a host of practical reasons, however, satirical forays of the kind remained sporadic into the 1820s. Cartoon historian Frank Weitenkampf counted merely seventy-eight American political caricatures prior to 1828—almost all of them handouts printed on individual pieces of paper and posted on some tavern wall or other public place. One reason for the scarcity of political cartoons was the laborious process of engraving figures on copper or cutting them into wood. Even when an artist was willing to do the work, he also expected to receive some compensation, and most newspaper and magazine publishers were so hard up for money that they made regular appeals to readers to donate rags to their paper mills. Moreover, the average daily newspaper had the severe layout problem of being committed to narrow columns, with the borders locking the type to the press's revolving cylinder; forced to choose between the inconvenience of opening up the columns on one page (and slowing down the printing of the entire paper) and squeezing a cartoon into one column, most publishers decided to stick to words. Lastly, it was commonplace at the time to rerun previously published cartoons for entirely different themes, with variations being confined to the captions. Artists had little room to complain about this practice because they were themselves in the habit of copying one another and selling their effort as personal inspiration. These practices helped both to popularize Franklin's "Join, or Die" and to insulate Revere against any great scandal when Pelham accused him of plagiarism.

Then came lithography—one of two nineteenth-century developments that wed political cartoons to the social reach and business calculations of the mass print media. Appropriately enough, the revolutionary surface printing method, which allowed for more detailed reproductions in a fraction of the time required previously, was effectively based on the mutual antagonism of oil and water. Introduced by Munich playwright Aloys Senefelder in 1796, lithography took some time to reach the United States because of patent squabbles, financial problems, and the priorities of such events as the War of 1812. Its eventual arrival on American shores was largely due to German and French immigrants. Its first known use in an American periodical came in the Philadelphia-based *Analectic Magazine* in July 1819—a mill scene by Bass Otis. But although regional maps and other handouts were produced in the intervening years, another decade had to pass before the technique was employed for a political cartoon. The work, printed by French immigrant Anthony Imbert, showed a map of the nation, over which Andrew Jackson's winning party in the form of a ravenous alligator in the West and John Quincy Adams's losing party in the guise of a tortoise in the East were engaged in a tail-tied tug-of-war.

Despite the production improvements introduced by the lithograph, for much of the rest of the century political cartoons remained more a feature of weekly and monthly magazines than of daily newspapers. Some artists weren't all that enthusiastic about the new process, already sensing that the quality of their work could be

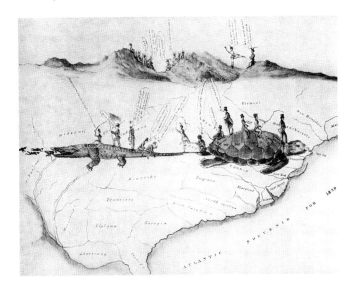

compromised by the haste for mass production runs. The first daily to take more than a passing stab at cartooning was the *United States Telegraph* of Washington in 1832, which did so primarily for the purpose of opposing Andrew Jackson's run for the presidency; illustrations were accompanied by jeering verse penned by Henry Ellenwood, who signed himself as Peter Pindar, Jr.[9] But it wasn't until 1867 that a significant publisher, James Gordon Bennett, Jr., of the New York *Evening Telegram*, printed editorial cartoons on a regular basis. A few years later, in 1873, New York's *Daily Graphic* became the first fully illustrated newspaper, but it still wasn't until the 1880s and 1890s that, with the help of such further technical advances as photoengraving, press barons Joseph Pulitzer and William Randolph Hearst incorporated illustrations on a steady basis, first in their Sunday editions and then as a daily feature.

The regular use of cartoons by daily newspapers has conditioned the genre to the present day. Once he signed a contract with a daily paper, the cartoonist, as never before, was expected to deliver his pictorial commentary not when the spirit moved him, but when the deadline did. Some artists—for reasons of temperament or principle—simply couldn't make the transition. Most of those who did more often than not found themselves submitting a toothless, vignette kind of humor they wouldn't have settled for in a less pressured working atmosphere. Long before the advertisers they would savor blaming for the same mentality, publishers knew that the fewer people they offended, the more of them would be likely to flag down a newsboy. Cartoonists were expected to know that and to draw the necessary conclusions.

2. Caricatures

Ralph Waldo Emerson thought a lot about caricatures. When he wasn't using the term to disparage somebody's grasp of a topic, he was praising the British magazine *Punch* for illustrations "equal to the best pamphlets, [conveying] to the eye in an instant the popular view which was taken of each turn of a public question." More direct on another occasion, he decided that "caricatures are often the truest history of the times."[10] While Emerson probably could have said something similar about tavern songs, his attention to the artistic form underlined how much it had established itself in the public consciousness by the nineteenth century.

In the United States, caricatures did not seriously assert their presence in cartoons until decades after the lithograph had made them a practical possibility. This was so despite the fact that Charles Philipon in France, for instance, had begun publishing such genre periodicals as *La Caricature* and *Le Charivari* by the early 1830s and Britain's *Punch* had followed in 1841. The closest to a stellar artistic presence over the first decades of the century was the Briton William Charles, who fled his homeland around 1806 after some of his artwork had too strenuously tested the virtue of forgiveness in local clergymen. Resettling in New York and then Philadelphia, Charles was particularly active during the War of 1812, turning out one engraving after another to celebrate American victories over the British. One of his bawdiest, "Queen Charlotte and Johnny Bull Get Their Dose of Perry," pictures a constipated-looking John Bull sitting on a commode while a crowned woman named for one of Admiral Oliver ("We have met the enemy and he is ours") Perry's ships sprays the names of the rest of the American fleet's units toward him after the battle of Lake Erie.

Throughout the middle years of the century, the prevailing cartoon motif was that of the successful lithographers Nathaniel Currier and James Merritt Ives; rather than distorting a subject's features, their customary approach to what passed for commentary was to depict realistically rendered public figures in some incongruous situation saying absurd things in balloons of dialogue. Physiognomies were usually so meticulous (not to say stiff) that the illustrators employed by Currier & Ives (as well as by Henry Robinson and similar houses) were presumed to have worked off daguerreotypes or photographs. Once caricature spread after the Civil War, though, cartoonists developed an almost visceral intimacy with the form. Whatever the given issue, their bold, judgmental strokes conveyed passions toward subjects (contempt was normally high on the list) as graphically suggestive as politically so. One historian noted this striking harmony in the most important figure in American cartooning, Thomas Nast. For Richard Samuel West, "Nast was a dogmatist, content to view the world as a struggle between good and evil. Consequently, his work was caustic and lecturing. The harshness of his heavy black line and the severity of his crosshatching mirrored his angry politics."[11]

However, there were almost as many criticisms of nineteenth-century editorial cartoons as artwork as there were politically tinged protests over perceived abuses of the individuals targeted by them. Among the irritated was the weekly *Nation* (which had its own agenda in glowering at competing periodicals):

The point in which caricature and especially American caricature almost universally fails is that of composition. The forlornly absurd pictures in our newspapers misnomered comic, in which public men are represented in impossible situations and doing impossible things, are like the vagaries and antics of postprandial dreams. The situations would be childish enough if they were correctly drawn; but to every impossibility of attitude is added the aggravation of linear distortion.[12]

A few years later, the same *Nation* was willing to grant that caricatures had their place, but only if executed by draftsmen of the rank of Carlo Pellegrini, a regular contributor to the British magazine *Vanity Fair*. "Would it be possible, we wonder, for some one of our illustrated journals to secure [Pellegrini] for a while?" the weekly asked. "He would be invaluable in a country where popular knowledge of the measures and policy of public men is necessarily slight, and in which the popular instinct for character might count for so much in shaping public opinion."[13]

The Nation overcame this aberrant moment in its good

judgment to go back to scoring illustrations, in daily newspapers as much as in magazines, until it accepted its own first cartoons after World War I. But even aside from that specific periodical, it wasn't really until journalism had made magazine illustrating a respectable career pursuit in the twentieth century that cartoonists escaped persistent jabs at their artistic abilities. Even among the British and Central European immigrants who dominated American cartoonist ranks in the nineteenth century, only an infinitesimal number were able to boast of formal training and experience. Although Nast would gain international recognition as a supreme artist, exerting a strong influence on (among others) Vincent van Gogh and Edgar Degas, even he was immersed in magazine illustration work by the age of fifteen. Adalbert Volck, the most gifted of the small handful of cartoonists who plumped for the South during the Civil War, had made his living as a dentist. Joseph Keppler, an Austrian immigrant who in 1876 founded the first successful humor weekly, *Puck*, first in German and then in English, had been an actor. The previous artistic experience of Homer Davenport, the chief pen in the turn-of-the-century Hearst empire, had been getting himself fired for his inability to draw a stove for an advertising company. The carping about the cartoonists' credentials was no trifle. A political intimidation ran through the aesthetic criticisms that, deliberate or not, chafed at the editorial credibility of the unschooled; i.e., if they hadn't acquired a firm enough grasp of the anatomical features they were lampooning, mightn't they simply be incompetent rather than satirical?

Numerous twentieth-century cartoonists, including Block, Feiffer, and Bill Mauldin, did have formal art training. But even before then, practically since Benjamin Franklin had realized he was slightly less proficient than William Hogarth, illustrators had managed to cope with the trauma of missing out on the academy; as often as not, they took pride in it, suggesting that their self-teaching was an indispensable component of their style. Some critics have held that it has been "the very artlessness" of cartoonists that "lay at the heart of their humor"; conversely, according to this perspective, the experience that makes a cartoonist a better draftsman as he matures also usually coincides with a dulling of his political passions, making him less potent as a graphic commentator overall.[14]

Rollin Kirby, whose early twentieth-century cartoons for the New York *World* earned him the first Pulitzer

Prize for his profession, echoed that sentiment when he told an interviewer that "a good idea has carried many an indifferent drawing to glory, but never has a good drawing rescued a bad idea from oblivion." According to Kirby, "every good cartoon is 75 percent idea and 25 percent drawing."[15] Herblock agreed, declaring that "the basic idea is the same as it ought to be with a written opinion—to try to say the right thing. Putting the thought into a picture comes second. . . . But the total cartoon is more important than just fun with faces and figures."[16] For historian Charles Press, "the political cartoon has always been an aesthetic achievement only by accident. Its purpose is propaganda, not art."[17] Press has also noted the reverse situation with superior nine-

OUR ARTIST'S OCCUPATION GONE.
TH: NAST. " It's all very funny to you; but what am I to do now?"

teenth-century draftsmen such as Frank Bellew. "Bellew fell short of starting a renaissance in political cartoons despite his artistic skills," the historian has drily observed, "because he had nothing in particular that he felt very excited by."[18]

The most accomplished nineteenth-century artists—Keppler and Nast—embodied the extremes of how to express excitement. By and large, Keppler's mode was sarcastic glee—first for German-language periodicals and an early German version of *Puck* (only the captions were translated into English) in St. Louis, then as a freelancer for (the weekly) *Frank Leslie's Illustrated Newspaper* and such monthlies as *Budget of Fun* and *Yankee Notions*, and finally as the guiding hand behind the New York–based English-language version of *Puck*. Nast, by contrast, seldom saw anything funny in what irritated him, and his satirical imagination was processed by razor blades. One of the byproducts of this outlook was a vulnerability to rival cartoonists. Whenever he took a particularly remonstrative or unorthodox position, as in his 1884 championing of Democratic presidential candidate Grover Cleveland, they couldn't wait to make him a caricature rather than a caricaturist. One recurring motif for such *Harper's Weekly* competitors as *Puck* was to picture Nast as a monkey working for his editor George Curtis the organ grinder. A June 28, 1884, drawing by Grant Hamilton on the cover of *Judge*, for example, had the monkey figure finishing the cartoon ("Too Heavy to Carry") with which the *Harper's Weekly* artist two weeks earlier had announced his support for Cleveland. Nast was also always in the sights of James Wales, an Ohio native who was one of the founders of *Judge* and had a claim to being the first homegrown U.S. cartoonist.

Much of this lampooning of Nast was based on envy, with some liberal sprinklings of jealousy. Alone among the major cartoonists of the period, Nast drew only what he was moved to draw for *Harper's Weekly*, having no editorial or ownership responsibilities. When he got into one of his periodic tangles with Curtis for contradicting what the magazine was proclaiming on its editorial page, he was able to count on the support of owner Fletcher Harper. When Harper died, Nast still refused to draw anything he didn't believe in, leading him to disappear from *Harper's* for months at a time because of the weekly's support of Rutherford B. Hayes and his own disdain for the president. By contrast, Keppler gradually took on the duties of an owner as much as the chief cartoonist of *Puck*, giving him a heightened appreciation of deadlines. In this double role he was often accused of swiping ideas from other staff members under publication pressures—a charge he usually laughed at in snorting *Puck* style.

The rancor toward Nast wasn't all jealousy. The "Prince of Caricaturists," as he billed himself on a national tour, had never been bashful about his achievements or reluctant to circulate in some of the same power circles he inveighed against on his own drawing board. The more he was celebrated, the less hesitant he was about dropping his own diminutive figure into his work—a red flag of self-importance contemporaries didn't miss (if only because many of them indulged the same habit). Needless to say, the Nast drawn by Nast had little in common with the savagely rendered squat rats and dwarves with goatees that appeared in *Puck*. By the time he was failing with his own *Nast's Weekly* (it lasted a mere five months in 1893), he had become only too

familiar as a cartoon character. Caricature's grotesqueries played no favorites.

3. Symbols

Those who hold that the Republican Elephant, the Democratic Donkey, and the Tammany Tiger are permanent features in the political circus take but a myopic view of our history, brief though it may be. We had politics and cartoons before any of these symbols was conceived and we may confidently expect the future will bring forth other singular graphic figurations born of the exigencies of the times and the imagination of the artist.[19]

William Murrell's 1935 prediction has gone largely unfulfilled. Republicans are still elephants, Democrats are still donkeys, and the political machines that have succeeded New York City's Tammany Hall haven't summoned forth any new animals from the cartoon bestiary. From start to finish, in fact, the twentieth century threw up few symbols of any kind with the durability of the creations of nineteenth-century cartoonists.

THE THIRD-TERM PANIC.

"An Ass, having put on the Lion's skin, roamed about in the Forest, and amused himself by frightening all the foolish Animals he met with in his wanderings."—SHAKESPEARE or BACON.

"THE TAMMANY TIGER LOOSE."—"What are you going to do about it?"

Early reliance on symbols (back to Franklin's snake in "Join, or Die") was hardly surprising. Symbols were an economic language in a frontier society where literacy wasn't always available currency. Whether borrowed from nature, religion, or mythology, they went a long way toward simplifying (when not precluding altogether) polemics through an appeal to a higher order. Caricatures, as damning as they could be, still carried the taint of mere human opinion, reflecting a cartoonist's situational attitude toward a subject; symbols sponsored the opinion as a deeper cultural assumption potential dissenters were more uneasy about disputing. It wasn't even necessary to advocate the symbol's propagandistic meaning to accept its hold, as British cartoonist James Gillray demonstrated on April 12, 1782, when he depicted the decisive surrender of Lord Cornwallis at Yorktown by showing Franklin's snake enwrapping British troops within its coils.

The positive image of the snake (reflected also in the "Don't Tread on Me" Navy Jack introduced in the fall of 1775) crested around the time of the Revolution, after which it largely fell into disuse one way or the other. Before then, in 1774, the serpent was cut into a ninth piece and bannered across the entire width of the front page of the Massachusetts *Spy* in emblematic combat with a British dragon. By 1860, however, with a bloc of southern states threatening secession and other states like Kansas ripped apart by the slavery issue, northern illustrators had come to see the creature only for its slimier attributes. One 1860 drawing entitled "Compromise Doctors" jeered at President James Buchanan's wretched role in feeding tensions in Kansas by picturing him as a woman at the bedside of a snake labeled Slavery and wailing to hovering quacks, "Doctor, my darling child is very sick. I have kindly nursed it for four years. I took it to Kansas for its health, but the vile inhabitants gave it a severe blow in the head." With similar imagery, northern Democrats cool to Abraham Lincoln's policies, especially the war against the South, came in for steady taunting as "copperheads"—a pejorative the party needed years to overcome.

Not all reptiles had to wait so long to be regarded balefully. From the beginning of the century, the snapping turtle was seen by pro-Federalist illustrators as the epitome of government oppression, most of all when it came to trade embargoes. An 1814 engraving by Alexander Anderson (from a sketch by John Jarvis) in the New York *Evening Post* pictures President James Madison severing a turtle's head—a reference to his submission to northeastern merchants who had demanded an end to mercantile restrictions against England. The period concern with the embargo issue also spawned a negative character known as the Ograbme—*embargo* backwards. One lyric at the time pledged that "[d]own to the grave t'atone for sin / Jemmy must go with Terrapin."[20] It was the identification of John Quincy Adams as a Federalist "traitor" who had supported the embargo that led to him being portrayed as a tortoise in the first lithographic political cartoon in 1828.

Besides his role in popularizing the snake as a patriotic symbol, Franklin made another—unintentional—contribution to cartoon vocabulary when his pet proposal for designating the turkey as the national bird got nowhere. Instead, there was the eagle, which gained iconic status when Charles Thomson, secretary of the Continental Congress, ended bickering among delegates over an appropriate design by putting it on the national seal in 1782. The bird made its first recorded appearance in a cartoon published shortly after John Adams had defeated Thomas Jefferson in the 1796 presidential elections. The work of a never-identified illustrator, "Providential Detection" portrays the anti-Federalist Jefferson worshiping at what is called the "Altar of Gallic Despotism" and being prevented from throwing

THE PROVIDENTIAL DETECTION

the Constitution into a fire of other revolutionary works by an American eagle. Under the eye of Providence, the eagle has used one of its talons to rescue the document from a blaze already consuming the writings of Paine, Voltaire, and fellow revolutionaries and is threatening Jefferson with the other claw. Falling from Jefferson's pocket is a controversial letter attacking Adams and George Washington as reactionaries that he had written to historian and confidant Philip Mazzei.

Despite its splashy debut, the eagle appeared irregularly as a national emblem for much of the rest of the nineteenth century and even then not always for conveying the nation's soaring aspirations. A double cartoon from 1861, for instance, was a before and after—the bird in full feather when handed to President Buchanan in 1857 and then plucked to misery by four years of what is identified as "Secession" and "Anarchy." It might have also been wilted by all the competition it had as a national symbol. For one cartoonist or another over the first half of the century, the United States was represented as Columbia, Brother Jonathan, Uncle Sam, and, more briefly, a Major Jack Downing; after them came two monuments—the Statue of Liberty and Abraham Lincoln. In one way or another, all of them replaced Yankee Doodle, a snide image of the colonists as coarse rubes attributed to Richard Schuckburg, a British army surgeon in the French and Indian War.

The plethora of national symbols spanning the human, animal, and mythological was inevitable for a fledgling republic seeking an identity. The first to lose significant purchase was Columbia. Columbia was something like a granddaughter of the British symbol Britannia, which was plastered on numerous enterprises in the colonies. In 1770, the Boston *Advertiser*, smarting after the Boston Massacre, took Britannia off its masthead in favor of the Greek goddess of war, Minerva. Minerva morphed into Columbia during the Revolution thanks in good part to Philip Freneau, the writer with claims to being one of the country's first working journalists and its oldest native white lyric poet. Following the 1775 Battle of Lexington, Freneau penned "American Liberty," whose verses include the couplet "What madness, Heaven, has made Britannia frown? / Who plans or schemes to pull Columbia down?"[21] The popularity of "American Liberty" among the colonists might have sufficed as the reason for the adoption of Columbia as a national symbol, but there have been other explanations as well. One of the more arcane has pointed to the prominence of the goddess in freemasonry lore and

accused Masons such as Freneau of devious maneuvers for imposing her on the national consciousness. However that might be, the graphically portrayed Columbia became increasingly obtrusive in its elusive combination of the ethereal and the sensual while the United States was persuading itself it was the land of the common man (underline *man*). She came across as especially awkward, and for more reasons than racism, when Nast and other cartoonists drew her alongside such ethnic stereotypes as Chinese coolies and Italian organ grinders.

Although Columbia has continued to appear on and off up to the present day, her symbolic role has long been overshadowed by the more stolid Statue of Liberty. (Minus the torch and the book, Columbia herself had been called "Liberty" long before F. A. Bartholdi's sculpture was dedicated in New York harbor in 1886.) One similarity between the two female figures is that they have usually been invoked for portraying the nation's values, while Uncle Sam has represented the government. A case in point was an 1899 illustration entitled "Army Beef Scandal" in which Columbia is shown complaining of a "disgusting and scandalous condition of affairs" and urging Sam to do something about it. As a rule, however, the inanimate implacability of Bartholdi's statue has marked a sharp turn away from the sandals, bare feet, or low-cut robes common to Columbia. Some drawings, such as an anonymous 1861 Currier & Ives piece, captured her in the crowd-leading, flag-waving kinds of charges more often associated with France's Marianne and other symbols of European revolution. Whatever her guise, there has seldom been much of the demure about Columbia.

As for Liberty, she got off to a bad start when Bartholdi displayed her right hand and torch at Philadelphia's Centennial Exhibition a good decade before the full statue was unveiled in New York. Between the frustrations sparked by this sneak peek and years of looking for financing for the statue's pedestal, cartoonists missed few opportunities to mock the enterprise. One anonymous drawing in the May 10, 1882, issue of *Puck* depicted Liberty as an old hag waiting for her plinth. In his "Warning Light: An Admonition of Pestilence and Death in Our Harbor" the previous April, Nast made her a figure of skeletal death in connection with street protests against Tammany Hall because of disease-spreading, uncollected garbage in the city. When the statue was finally installed, F. Victor Gillam's "Erecting the New York Political Statue" in the September 4, 1886, *Judge* focused on corrupt wardheelers carrying off its various parts.

LET THE ADVERTISING AGENTS TAKE CHARGE OF THE BARTHOLDI BUSINESS, AND THE MONEY WILL BE RAISED WITHOUT DELAY.

As Roger Fischer and others have pointed out, Liberty's reign in the national imagination as a symbol of freedom hasn't stopped cartoonists from suffering some curious blackouts. Speaking about the iconic status achieved by the statue by World War I, Fischer noted in his *Them Damned Pictures* that "her evolution into a generic symbol of American patriotism was so nearly complete by then that she was rarely if ever invoked against wartime and postwar suppressions of civil liberties and the push to curtail the flow of 'huddled masses' into the United States—both blatant mockeries of ideals she had been created to symbolize!"[22] The same was pretty much true of the next Red Scare in the 1950s, not to mention the civil rights abuses shielded by the Patriot Act in the new millennium. Conversely, countless artists

A DISGUSTING AND SCANDALOUS CONDITION OF AFFAIRS.

over the years have responded to black national moments with the quick fix of showing the female Liberty in tears.

Brother Jonathan started life as a bumpkin stage character barely beyond Yankee Doodle on the evolutionary scale (among other things, he retained Doodle's feather in his cap). A tall, shrewd New Englander with a smart mouth and incarnations as a trader, peddler, and seaman, he ranked honesty pretty far down on his list of best policies. He was always the People as opposed to the Government, going out of his way to hoodwink the latter (though he didn't mind taking advantage of anybody at all). That wasn't uplifting enough for illustrators like Amos Doolittle, who drafted him for patriotic purposes, most prominently during the War of 1812. One Doolittle engraving from October 21, 1813, shows Jonathan forcing Yankee grog down the throat of John Bull, who whines that he would prefer Holland gin, French brandy, or anything else not American. It was through cartoons of the kind that Brother Jonathan was "rehabilitated" as an American hero. The conversion didn't do much for his obnoxiousness. In an 1846 illustration by Edward W. Clay, for example, the cheroot-smoking, swaggering Jonathan is depicted as kicking General Santa Anna away from Texas with the words, "You come to steal away my new boot? I'll discumgalligumfriate you!" For his part, Doolittle defended his reworking of Jonathan's stage character as being in the interests of "inspiring our countrymen with confidence in themselves and eradicating any terrors that they may feel as respects the enemy they have to combat."[23]

Brother Jonathan's time ran out around the Civil War, when his long-tailed blue coat and red-and-white

BROTHER JONATHAN *Administering* a *Salutary Cordial to* JOHN BULL.

striped trousers were passed on to Uncle Sam. The most widely retailed version of Sam's origins track him to a Troy, New York, meat packer named Samuel Wilson who supplied the army during the War of 1812 and who stamped his shipments with a big *U.S.*; in this telling, it was some warehouse worker or wagon loader who was the first to joke that he was handling provisions from Uncle Sam. In 1961, Congress was sufficiently impressed by the story to pass a resolution declaring Wilson "the progenitor of America's national symbol." If nothing else, that put paid to discomforting speculation that the source of the figure had actually been the nineteenth-century circus clown Dan Rice, who had done his act in a goatee, top hat, blue leotard, and red and white tights.

Although Sam followed Brother Jonathan as the most prevalent national symbol, the succession wasn't all that neat. One of the more memorable illustrations from 1876, Frank Bellew's "Imperialism Cartoon," shows a Sam-like figure explicitly identified as Jonathan and a Russian named Ivan struggling to hold on to the globe as they both reach for Asia. On the other hand, and contrary to long-held assertions that he didn't appear in cartoons until shortly before the Civil War, Sam was already around in the 1830s as a Jonathan contemporary, if without the goatee and his familiar hat and costume. In an unsigned 1834 piece captioned "Uncle Sam in Danger," he was depicted as an ailing man surrounded by four quacks—President Andrew Jackson, Vice-President Martin Van Buren, presidential advisor Amos Kendall, and Missouri Senator Thomas Hart Benton. Three years later, with "Uncle Sam Sick with La Grippe," most of the same characters were back in the same setting for another graphic screed on how the Democrats were imperiling the country by refusing to recharter the national bank; this time there was the added background presence of Jonathan, shown to be greeting the equivalent of a legitimate doctor, bank president Nicholas Biddle. "La Grippe" is the only documented instance of the two symbols costarring in a panel.

Sam's rise to dominance during the Civil War was not without its ironies. While Nast and other northern illustrators gradually incorporated Lincolnesque features into his figure, they were not the first to do so. That vision came from two Britons—Matt Morgan in *Fun* magazine and John Tenniel in *Punch*—who were actually being critical of the sixteenth president for his attempts to keep the Union together. Although Morgan and Tenniel found it natural to give Sam a Lincoln-like set of whiskers, the later use of a white goatee has variously been ascribed to Nast, Keppler, and C. G. Bush, another cartoonist for *Harper's Weekly*. What has come to be regarded as the definitive representation of Sam—the 1916 "I WANT YOU" from the cover of *Frank Leslie's Illustrated Weekly Newspaper*—was the work of James Montgomery Flagg, who used himself as a model. The magazine cover was subsequently used as a recruiting poster in both World War I and World War II. In the event, this turned out to be the height of Sam's emblematic career. In recent decades, cartoonists have habitually invoked him in a burlesque vein, suggesting nothing so much as the kind of circus man on stilts who once worked with the forgotten Dan Rice.

Before Uncle Sam came along, Brother Jonathan had to scuffle for the limelight with Major Jack Downing—in fact, with more than one Major Jack Downing. Downing was the creation of Maine writer Seba Smith, whose fictitious *Life and Writings of Major Jack Downing of Downingville* in 1830 introduced the character of a rustic Yankee defender of the policies of Andrew Jackson. The Major was too colorful not to inspire cartoonists, especially around Jackson's decision not to recharter the National Bank and the vehement response that brought from the opposition Whigs. Numerous lithographers put out prints, many of them signed by the Major's fictional "Neffu." In the "Downfall of Mother Bank" (1833), Downing is pictured as standing behind Jackson watching the walls come down on bank president Biddle, Whig leaders Henry Clay and Daniel Webster, and the kind of pro-bank newspapers that delighted in the "La Grippe" cartoon with Uncle Sam and Jonathan. In another, he is shown cheering on Jackson as the president and Biddle square off in a boxing match in the middle of a field. A third portrays him leading Jackson back to bed after the president has had a violent nightmare about Biddle.

But the pro-Jackson Downing wasn't the only one available for a few pennies in the 1830s. Spurred on by newspaperman Charles August Davis, a friend of Biddle's, lithographers also marketed anti-Jackson fare featuring the Major. In "This Is the House That Jack Built," for instance, the President's Kitchen Cabinet is depicted as a pack of rats gorging on public deposits; the anonymous cartoonist presented Downing as a soldier with a rooster's head holding up a flag that reads "Jackson and Glory." Although Jackson was back to private life by 1837 and dead by 1845, the Major went on—not as conceived by Smith, but as counterconceived by cartoonists following the Davis promptings. As late as 1862, Bromley & Co. issued "The Grave of the Union—A Major Jack Downing Dream Drawn by Zeke" (a variation on the "Neffu"). The lithograph shows Lincoln and his chief aides as undertakers burying the Constitution—a widely held view following the passage of the Conspiracies Act that suspended habeas corpus and jailed almost forty thousand people on the flimsiest of pretexts. It was only after the war that Downing was retired from the scene altogether.

Under the sway of opponents like Davis, Major Jack

joined Uncle Sam and Brother Jonathan as cartoon tools for making the populist Jackson look bad; whatever the pretensions to designing national symbols, it wasn't an ambition burdened by nonpartisanship. If not the very first, the relentless attacks by cartoonists on Jackson and his administration were an important early example of how northeastern media centers conditioned impressions of what vox populi was saying across the country. Certainly, any study of the political illustrations by such stalwarts of the period as Edward Williams Clay, David Claypoole Johnston, and James Akin gave little indication that Old Hickory, after barely losing in 1824 due to an eleventh-hour back-room deal, not only won the 1828 election resoundingly, but was reelected by an even greater margin four years later.

One of the most enduring legacies of Jackson and his fractious critics was the Democratic donkey. As in the case of George Washington and the vanished 1789 piece called "The Entry," the animal appealed to illustrators for its jackass connotations. Jackson trumped that sally, however, by making the donkey an election campaign symbol of his own, playing up his mule-like dedication and stubbornness in fighting for his policies. That took a lot of the bray out of illustrators, at least until after the Tennessean had left the White House. But then in 1837, with the retired Jackson still trying to call the shots for his party, the anonymously authored "The Modern Balaam and His Ass" showed the former president vainly urging his party (the ass) to move in the direction he wanted. "Balaam" marked the real start of the donkey symbol for the Democrats.

Although frequently credited with originating the donkey idea, Nast came to it decades later and only after

THE BRITISH LION AND THE BENGAL TIGER.

he had been in the habit of viewing Democrats as foxes—an allusion not only to the animal's fabled slyness but also to Martin Van Buren, Jackson's successor as president, who was known to many as "the Fox" for the same quality. His first documented use of the donkey didn't come until 1869, when "A Live Jackass Kicking a Dead Lion" portrayed the supposed reaction of Democrats to the death of Republican Secretary of War Edwin Stanton. On the other hand, Nast did sire the Republican elephant. If the Democratic donkey was born in censure, the Republican elephant was the product of a trial balloon and a hoax in 1874. The trial ballon consisted of indications that Grant was contemplating running for an unprecedented third term—a step denounced by (among others) the New York *Herald* as "Caesarian" in its arrogance. Around the same time, the New York daily gained national attention for splashing a sensational story across its front page claiming that wild animals had escaped from the Central Park Zoo and were prowling Manhattan in search of prey. In the immediate widespread panic over the report, few readers noticed a small footnote from editor Thomas Connery admitting that the story was false and was aimed at underlining the woeful maintenance conditions at the zoo—making it the nineteenth-century equivalent of Orson Welles's 1939 radio broadcast about the Martian invasion of Earth.

On November 7, Nast, who rarely needed a reason to defend Grant, combined the two stories in *Harper's Weekly* to show rampaging animals, including an elephant with the words "The Republican Vote." An ass (Democrats) is depicted frightening the other beasts, and none more than the elephant, a symbol of Republican voters rather than the party itself. The moral was, "If you believed the zoo story, you'll believe this one, too." (In fact, though, Grant *had been* harboring third-term thoughts—so much so that in 1875, seventy-six years before Congress passed the Twenty-second Amendment, a fearful Senate approved a resolution announcing its opposition to any third terms. Not even that prevented Grant's cronies from seeking a third term for him in 1880.)

Jackson aside, neither party was quick to embrace its cartoon animal. For a while, Democratic organizations in the South preferred the rooster for its suggestions of alertness. What no Democrat wanted to be identified with was another creation associated with Nast—the Tammany tiger.

The first source for the Tammany tiger was an 1857 *Punch* illustration by Tenniel entitled "The British Lion's Vengeance on the Bengal Tiger," a depiction of the Kanpur Mutiny in India. Then there was the fire engine company where Nast's most famous target, political boss William Tweed, had once worked; the fire station's lead wagon had carried a tiger's head as an emblem—a souvenir Tweed had taken with him as he had climbed the political ladder. But maybe more of a midwife than anything for the Nast drawing of November 15, 1871, was a Keppler piece that had appeared a mere three weeks earlier (October 22, 1871) in the German-English St. Louis version of *Puck*. Double-captioned as "Who Will Conquer?" and "*Wer Wird Siegen?*" the Keppler cartoon shows Columbia fighting in an arena with a tiger wearing a collar labeled "Corruption" and was clearly a reference to the turmoil then under way in New York over the Tweed gang. As for Nast, he had used a tiger's head earlier in various attacks on Tweed, but waited until two days before New York's 1871 municipal elections to spring the whole animal in "The Tammany Tiger Loose—What Are You Going to Do about It?" As much as it might have owed to Tenniel and Keppler, the startling double-page depiction of the cat in a Roman arena about to chew up a fallen Columbia was far more powerful. Although even more instrumental than *Harper's Weekly* in the downfall of Tweed and the Democrats, the *New York Times* wasn't alone in calling the cartoon "the most impressive political picture ever produced in this country."

As for the Republicans, they weren't so enthusiastic about the elephant, either, and sought for awhile to think of themselves as other noble creatures, especially the eagle. Eventually, however, they came around to adopting the elephant as an official party symbol—a step the Democrats have never taken with the donkey. For a brief period in the 1880s, there was another party animal—the bull. It was one of two emblems of the Independent Party promoted by Keppler and his *Puck* partner Adolph Schwarzmann as an alternative to Republicans and Democrats. Even more visible in *Puck* cartoons for several years was the Independent Voter—a figure in a red shirt, boots, and slouch hat who carried around an axe for destroying the political corruption embodied by the two standing parties.

Since the World War I years, the Statue of Liberty has had its male equivalent in Abraham Lincoln. The centerpiece of the Lincoln mythology has been Daniel Chester French's sculpture of the sixteenth president within the Lincoln Memorial in Washington's Potomac Park. For the most part, cartoonists have depicted the monumental Lincoln presiding regally over American strength and virtue, betraying nothing on its countenance but a hint that those turned toward him think again about what they're doing. But there have been several conspicuous exceptions. In an April 1990 issue of the Tacoma *Morning News*, Steve Benson stripped Lincoln to an undershirt and polkadot shorts over a legend "Four Score and Several Hundred Billion Dollars Ago" to make a point about Washington's extravagant spending. But the most memorable use of the memorial statue was unquestionably Mauldin's November 22, 1963, illustration for the Chicago *Sun-Times* showing Lincoln grieving over the assassination of John F. Kennedy. Aside from eschewing the triter option of having the Statue of Liberty crying, the Mauldin cartoon underlined Lincoln's twin symbolic role of values *and* government, both of them overcome by the Dallas killing.

As the open frontiers of the nineteenth century closed down to the urban grids of the twentieth, cartoonists had even less reason to seek a symbol of the People in a gadding, rambunctious character like Brother Jonathan. Rather, they found it in various figures that seemed perennially suspended between bewilderment that their left pants pocket had been picked and dread that the right one was about to go next. The most continuous of these characters were Frederick Burr Opper's Mr. Common Man, introduced for the Hearst chain during the 1900 presidential election race between William McKinley and William Jennings Bryan, and Vaughn Shoemaker's John Q. Public, created some thirty years later for the Chicago *Daily News*. Even starker was a representative Taxpayer first drawn by Will Johnstone of the New York *World Telegram* in 1933; as conceived by Johnstone and copied by a myriad of others, the Taxpayer was reduced to wearing a barrel for clothing. None of these Everymen doubted that Uncle Sam was the government and not them or that the donkeys and elephants were primarily interested in their own feeding times. Opper's character probably reached its peak in "An Alphabet of Joyous Trusts," a stunning tour de force in which the cartoonist came up with a trust industry for all twenty-six letters and depicted each as stomping all over Mr. Common Man.

The Opper, Shoemaker, and Johnstone creations marked a cleavage that, in the name of the same populist spirit that had been detested during the Jackson era, victimistically played up the bafflements of living in a mass society. In a reflection of the the third-person narratives of the comic strip, they also carried a subtle shift in voice in which the cartoonist delegated commentaries to a buffer figure more regularly than in the past. It was Nast who whacked Tweed directly (even boastfully), but it was the Taxpayer, not Will Johnstone, who was being whacked by federal taxes.

4. Words

It took some time for American cartoonists to accept that a picture was worth a thousand words. To be on the safe side, well up to the threshold of the twentieth century, they continued to jam words into, around, and under their work. Rare was the caricature that didn't come with a name tag, brand stamp, or ballooned remark; rarer still the cartoon panel that didn't look like an exercise in comparative calligraphy. About the only thing allowed to speak for itself was the caption. Nast epitomized this practice to a sardonic degree with his July 1, 1876, *Harper's Weekly* cartoon "Tweed-le-dee and Tilden-dum," posing Tweed before a facsimile of the various type sizes on the front page of the periodical itself. Keppler didn't think Nast was in any position to be ironic; according to the *Puck* editor, Nast's cartoons often resembled "a chapter from the Patent Office Reports."[24]

What all the verbiage underscored was that political cartooning was not the same thing as pure caricature, that it was always addressing itself to specific questions —not to Abraham Lincoln, but to Abraham Lincoln suspending habeas corpus; not to William McKinley, but to William McKinley's love affair with the business trusts. The more complex the issue, the less familiar its chief actors, the wordier cartoonists (or their employers) were prone to become in order to make sure an illustration's point of view was communicated. Another determining factor was the cartoon medium. One-shot engravings nailed to an oak tree at the beginning of the century were seldom crafted elaborately enough to be self-explanatory; midcentury lithographs sold as freestanding pieces from bookstores and barber shops usually needed contexts spelled out, as well. The heavier use of allegorical symbols—many alluding to literary sources (Shakespeare, Aesop, *The Arabian Nights*) not as much in

vogue among the minimally educated as once upon a time—also increased insecurities about elliptical messages, prompting captions within captions.

On the other hand, it wasn't only for their talent that cartoonists working toward the end of the century repeatedly drew praise for their greater "power" and "forcefulness." The deadlines imposed by working for daily newspapers left far less time for crowd scenes, contributing to an overall sparer look visually; in turn, especially with the advent of photoengraving for reproductions, the clearer fields made for a much more commanding effect. Those working for a daily publication also had the reasonable expectation that viewers had run their eyes across a headline in another part of the journal, relieving them of some of their didacticism. Beyond that, the newspaper-buying habit itself made it superfluous for cartoonists to introduce themselves and their pet peeves to regular readers in pedantic detail every morning of the week. Finally, but no less important for both cartoonists and consumers, photography had begun shaping different viewing instincts: If Mathew Brady didn't need crossword puzzle clutter to express a point, why did Joseph Keppler?

Not all the words in the early years were mere directional arrows; some were the entire raison d'être of the cartoon. This was markedly so where anemic puns were concerned, and such public figures as George Fox, Hamilton Fish, Elihu Root, and Thurlow Weed were given every reason to come to despise their surnames. Cartoonists reserved a special place in their hell for Lewis Cass, the 1848 Democratic presidential candidate and secretary of state in the later Buchanan administration: not too many days went by when he wasn't reminded that his name rhymed with *ass* and *gas.* Equally strained were the in-panel conversations between figures when a lithographer's motif came from the sports world. A Lincoln political victory inevitably meant goading some background character into saying Abe had hit a home run, crossed the finished line first, or run the pool table; worse, that character's poetics elicited a response from a second character with his own collection of weary metaphors.

The deemphasis on words over the second half of the nineteenth century has sometimes come wrapped within the insinuation that the trend was hastened by a calculated dumbing-down appeal to the illiterate and newly arrived immigrants, particularly the English-speaking Irish. Exhibit one for this claim has been the reputed outburst by Tweed after he had seen Nast's "'Twas Him" cartoon in the August 19, 1871, issue of *Harper's Weekly* accusing the Tammany Hall leader of stealing public money. "Stop them damn pictures,"

Tweed was alleged to have ordered his henchmen. "I don't care so much what the papers write about me. My constituents can't read. But, damn it, they can see pictures."[25]

At best, the quotation is apocryphal; more plausibly, it was fumes from the prejudice rampant in Republican circles against the Irish and other immigrants who comprised the core of the Democratic Party's popular support and who later laid out their pennies for Pulitzer's New York *World* and Hearst's New York *Journal.* The condescension historically reserved for the latter two papers has obscured the fact that the supposedly tonier *Harper's Weekly* and the *New York Times,* were concocting stories out of thin air long before Pulitzer and Hearst were applying themselves to that task. In the words of one writer, they "fabricated descriptions, invented scandals, or published long interviews that no lips ever emitted."[26] Even Keppler's *Puck,* regarded as a crest for political cartooning during the so-called Gilded Age, often went to perverse lengths to live up to its slogan of "What Fools We Mortals Be." It found nothing wrong in routinely depicting the Irish and African Americans as fellow apes, as in Opper's March 19, 1884, illustration "Gorilla Warfare under the Protection of the American Flag." And this despite the fact that Keppler, for all his protestations of being completely independent, regularly endorsed Democrats, the supposed party of the immigrants.

However many illiterates there might have been in the United States toward the end of the nineteenth century (and there were decidedly fewer every day), it is doubtful that a majority of them were within the middle and upper middle classes that accounted for the read-

lican well-to-do about who was and who wasn't an igno-ramus. It also didn't appeal as much to Keppler, who, while a Democrat, liked nothing more than using his chromolithograph printing to fill *Puck* with characters wearing garish green pants. Happily for the cartoonist, there was one ethnic group that was particularly associated with the color green.

For its part, the penny press of Pulitzer and Hearst, while definitely equating circulation with the economically taxed, also had more urgent political and business agendas than turning out daily coloring books for the illiterate. If their cartoons were stripped to essentials, so were their news stories, with facts usually regarded as among the first luxuries to go. Where cartoons suited such sensationalist dailies as the *World* or the *Journal* was in providing single dramatic images for the newspaper's general slant on an issue or event. For the Pulitzer paper, that especially meant supporting the news-making publicity stunts (Nellie Bly's 1889 circling of the globe, for example) that the daily sponsored on a regular basis; for the Hearst organ, it meant reinforcing the agitprop of the moment, including anything related to the publisher's own political ambitions. That cartoonists like Opper and Davenport played along was a condition of their employment, not a strategy for building bridges to, or even patronizing, the latest Paddy or Gino off the boat. The overriding priority of the penny press, as with any other daily, was collecting as many pennies as possible, from wherever. Sometimes even cheapskate contractual conditions generated its cartoons. At Pulitzer's *World*, for example, most reporters were paid by the inch rather than by a fixed salary; this motivated writers like James Stuart Blackton, the future founder of the

ership of *Harper's Weekly*. If Tweed worried about his street sweepers, longshoremen, and delivery boys seeing Nast's hideous caricatures of him and his cronies in the periodical, it wasn't because that rank and file subscribed to it in great numbers or couldn't wait to dip into a tight family budget to buy a copy to see how he had been ridiculed. Where the Tammany Hall chief would have far more likely feared reverberations was in the established network of business and political liaisons (including a lot of upstate Republicans) that kept his clique functioning—white-collar workers and professionals who had more options than the piecemeal work and handouts grandly bestowed on recently transplanted Europeans. But that influence network didn't lend itself as easily to preconceptions among the Repub-

Vitagraph motion picture studio, to submit stories (most of them also fiction) with elaborate illustrations.[27] The picture wasn't just worth a thousand words; it was worth a few more bucks.

At various junctures in cartoon history, the picture has also *been* the word. The first noteworthy meeting between political cartoons and the dictionary took place in England in 1843, when the word *cartoon* itself gained its contemporary meaning. Up to then, it had signified only a rough sketch for a painting or fresco. But when the British government sponsored a show of paintings commissioned to beautify the houses of Parliament, the humor magazine *Punch* led the charge in decrying the waste of money. It published a John Leech illustration showing a ragtag crowd of the needy and crippled looking bewildered by the framed oils of upper-class twits and pampered animals, commenting, "The poor ask for bread and the philanthropy of the State accords an exhibition."[28] The magazine entitled the Leech work "Cartoon No. 1."

Cartooning contributions to language in America began in the nineteenth century, when a print of the Union showed Pennsylvania in the middle, making it the Keystone State from that point on. More noted was the March 12, 1812, illustration that appeared in the Boston *Gazette* and introduced the word *gerrymander.* Inspired by Massachusetts Governor Elbridge Gerry's decision to realign the voting district of Essex County to ensure reelection, Elkanah Tilsdale reconfigured the state map into a giant salamander that his editor dubbed "The Gerry-mander—a new species of Monster." The Tilsdale piece is widely regarded as the first American cartoon where wit was equal to the political point being made.

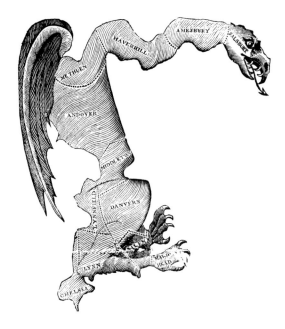

In 1902, Washington *Post* cartoonist Clifford Berryman accompanied President Theodore Roosevelt on a trip for settling a border dispute between Mississippi and Louisiana. During a hunting break from the talks on November 11, Roosevelt rejected the opportunity to shoot a tied-up bear cub for publicity purposes, and Berryman's "Drawing the Line in Mississippi" featured the animal that would soon be commercialized around the world as a teddy bear. In 1924, Harold Tucker Webster, known to admirers as the "Mark Twain of cartoonists," drew a strip in New York for the *World* and then the *Herald Tribune* called "The Timid Soul" that revolved around a character named Caspar Milquetoast. Ever since, mild-mannered, ineffectual men prone to being dominated have dreaded being known as milquetoasts. In 1931, the humor magazine *Ballyhoo* made one of its motifs the response of characters to an unseen figure outside the cartoon panel; because the invisible man's name was Joe Zilch, that has been generally accepted as the origin of the word *zilch* to mean "nothing."

Another conspicuous contribution to language came on the heels of Wisconsin Senator Joseph McCarthy's February 1950 lies that he had ferreted out a nest of communists in the State Department. Soon afterward, on March 29, Herblock's "You Mean I'm Supposed to Stand on That?" for the Washington *Post* depicted Republican leaders in Congress trying to drag a fearful elephant to a shaky tower of mud-filled buckets labeled "McCarthyism." Ever since, the term has denoted coordinated repressive measures feeding off fear and bluster. The more speciously applied term *politically correct* owed much of its early dissemination to cartoons drawn by Jeff Shesol, a Brown University senior in the late 1980s who later took his character of Thatch, the Politically Correct Man, to the Washington *Post*. For personal

SELF-EMPTYING ASH TRAY OF THE FUTURE

Bright Romantic moon brings love birds (A) together on perch (B), causing string (C) to upset sprinkling can (D) and wet shirt (E). Shirt shrinks, unveiling portrait (F). Dog (G), seeing portrait of his master, wags tail, brushing ashes from tray into asbestos bag (H). Smoldering butts ignite rocket (I) which carries bag of ashes out the window into the far reaches of the sky.

This should encourage young couples to start families, because the children can wear the shrunken shirts.

identification, though, nobody has matched Rube Goldberg, who took up political cartooning for the New York *Sun* in 1938 after years of turning out graphic comic series. It was during this former phase of his career that he began drawing hopelessly complex machines that performed idiotically simple tasks in convoluted ways. Dictionaries now define accomplishing something simple in a roundabout way as a Rube Goldberg.

5. Stereotypes

American cartooning's sorry history on ethnic and racial stereotyping has sometimes been made to look like an inevitable accompaniment to editorial caricaturing. Abetting this perspective is the fact that the genre's trumpeted golden age in the late nineteenth century was also a period of virulently bigoted illustrations, unmatched in volume and scurrility except during the two world wars and in their immediate aftermaths. A fanciful variation on this outlook assumes that the kind of choleric personality often attracted to editorial cartooning would be too instinctively intemperate to worry about bruising sensitivities; i.e., idiosyncratic geniuses can't always be judged by normal standards. Both attitudes not only seek to rationalize the historical record but also underestimate the variety of stereotypes invoked for polemical ends. In fact, those of an ethnic and racial kind were not the only coarse manifestations of Feiffer's "ill will" on the doorstep of the twentieth century. On any number of levels, the period saw not merely an explosion of the creative extravagances of caricature's "truthful misrepresentations" but also a decided

"WHAT ARE YOU LAUGHING AT? TO THE VICTOR BELONG THE SPOILS."

been born into in his native Germany and that he had later abandoned with a vengeance. This led the publishers and the cartoonist to find common fury in such New York City issues as the easing of compulsory Protestant lessons in public schools (where reading the King James Bible was considered a "secular" activity) and in a Tweed-backed state bill helping to fund Catholic parochial schools. But if these factors provided pertinent political and psychological grounding for years of attacks on the Democratic city administration, it wasn't until July 21, 1871, when the *New York Times* laid out in detail the millions in payoffs and other frauds attached to the municipality's building of a courthouse and other public works projects, that Nast had the smoking gun for his ruinous *political* stereotype of Tammany Hall.

Previously, he had tried more traditional profiling. Among other things, he had depicted Tweed and the rest of the Tammany crew as Indians on the warpath and as Irish Alley Oops. None of these had made much of an impression, if only because none of the targeted Democrats had Indian blood and only a couple of the most visible leaders ("Brains" Sweeney and "Slippery Dick" Connolly) were Irish. But in the wake of the *Times* disclosures, he came up with the single image of Tweed that he had been seeking—not because the party leader and state senator was the first among equals, not because he was Irish or Catholic (he was neither), but because the long banana nose, beard, and beady eyes tacked on to his bulbous torso made him the most likely Democrat to excite revulsion from *Harper's Weekly* readers—what British art historian Ernst Gombrich has called "mythologiz(ing) the world by physiognomizing it." Put more simply, Tweed was the easiest man in the Demo-

pandering to the ticking demands of settled prejudices. Whether it was *Harper's Weekly* or the New York *World*, catering to readers seemed like a good idea.

Even without the Irish immigrants whose attachment to Tammany Hall played on his nerves, Nast's campaign against Tweed was destined to dip into crudity. The periodical he worked for, *Harper's Weekly*, had arrived at its niche in the Republican Establishment only after its owners had banged the drum for years for Know-Nothing nativism and had profited handsomely from distributing xenophobic hate literature; one of their biggest sellers, written by a former monk, had relished scenes of nuns knifing priests. The Catholicism abhorred by the Harpers was also the religion that Nast had cratic ruling circle to draw as a menace, and Nast did that drawing for what has been called the "defining moment" of American cartoon history fifty-odd times over the second half of 1871 (with as many as six pieces in the *Harper's* issue published a mere two days before that year's city elections).

But even the obsessive portrayal of Tweed as bloated arrogance and venality would have remained standard caricature if Nast hadn't tossed in an extra or two to be sure *Harper's* readers responded not just to his art but also to their own preconceptions about the last word in viciousness and degeneracy. One favorite trick, for instance, was to identify the politician in several illustrations as William *Marcy* Tweed despite the fact that his middle name wasn't Marcy, but Magear. Why Marcy? Because William Marcy was the Jacksonian Democrat from New York State who, in the early 1830s, had taken the U.S. Senate floor to proclaim "to the victor belong the spoils"—an apt sentiment for the panels of dissolution and corruption to which Tweed had been sentenced by Nast. Like the most effective stereotype aids, this detail wasn't spelled out for explicit sarcasm, where it might have been only a one-time japery; through repetition it was allowed to go on tickling the reader's assumptions about greed and profligacy. So successful was the name alteration ploy that to this day encyclopedias and history texts continue to identify Tweed with the middle name of Marcy.

Not that awareness has always been much of a remedy, either. After a century and a half, for example, the malevolent physiognomizing of Tweed has become transparent to many commentators, but these have then gone to the revisionist extreme of suggesting that the patronage boss, state senator, third biggest owner of Manhattan real estate, occupant of a Fifth Avenue mansion and Greenwich, Connecticut, estate, breeder of horses, and captain of two yachts was no more powerful than other Tammany stalwarts of his time. This would have come as a surprise to the thousands who reelected him in 1871 even as all his cronies were failing in reelection bids in the wake of the *Times* revelations and the Nast cartoons. It also would have implicated the judicial system in a persecutorial campaign in light of the twelve-year jail sentence Tweed was later given for a corruption conviction, a flight from the United States before additional charges, and his eventual death in a prison cell. Nearer the truth is that, even after all this time, Nast's contrivances have remained vaguely discomfiting for many. Brilliant as they might have been propagandistically and artistically, they also pose all those messy questions about the difference between the outrageous and the unethical, about when the means justify the ends, and about the validity of accusations made by people with partisan interests—intellectual intrigues that rarely produce pure heroes and pure villains even in "defining moments."

Tweed wasn't the only political stereotype on drawing boards in the waning years of the nineteenth century. Another was William Alfred Peffer, whose obscurity today would have been matched by that in his own time except for the cartoonists of *Puck* and *Judge*. As Fischer has described the Kansas Populist, "Odd man out in a two-party chamber, Peffer left no great legacy of note from his 1891–97 stint in the U.S. Senate, save perhaps a wealth of speeches in the *Congressional Record* distinguished mainly by their interminable length and plethora of statistics."[29] A Peffer contemporary agreed, saying he was "as devoid of personal magnetism as a hitching post."[30] But none of this prevented the Democratic-leaning *Puck* (over its infatuation with the need for a third national party) and the Republican-leaning *Judge* from devoting an estimated sixty cartoons to him while the senator was droning on in the Upper House. His cachet? Not that he was a Populist and that, if they couldn't agree on anything else, *Puck* and *Judge* were united in wanting to safeguard the two-party system against outsiders; there were plenty of more famous Populists around for that. What Peffer had going for him that a James Weaver and a William Jennings Bryan didn't were a long, straggly beard and burning eyes that stirred unpleasant associations with John Brown's bloody rampage in Kansas before the Civil War and with the more recent violent activities of anarchists and revolutionaries in Europe. That Peffer gave little indication of even knowing what a bomb was was neither here nor there. For the eastern magazines, his beard and eyes made the Populists a disturbance to the natural order of a Democratic-Republican nation, his Kansas background made clear why rubes should be seen and not heard in a New York–ruled world, and the whole package made him a source of hilarity in the universe.

Sometimes, the cartoonists even came close to acknowledging their tactics, as in C. J. Taylor's "Old Jokes in New Political Clothes," published by *Puck* on January 30, 1895. In this cartoon the scruffy Peffer is shown entering the Senate with a satchel bursting with Wild Ideas and Populist Dreams. The caption says, "The Amusing Political Hayseed—His intellect is very ordinary, but his whiskers are the wonder of the country." Before they

were through with him, *Puck* and *Judge* seeded (totally unfounded) conjecture that Peffer would be the Populist presidential candidate in 1892 and 1896—an excuse for putting his rug-long beard in more illustrations.

Enlightened by the right muse, nineteenth-century cartoonists could stoop to religious stereotypes without indicting a specific ethnic group in the bargain. Although the Irish were usually hovering in the wings, for example, Nast went after the papacy without explicit Hibernian help on several occasions. On February 19, 1870, he contributed a double panel to *Harper's Weekly* in which he contrasted the power situations of Catholics in Europe and the United States. In the first panel, the

pope is shown fainting away as the divinity Europa rips up a church-state quilt to the general approval of the continent's chiefs-of-state; in the second one, American Catholics are represented as sewing the quilt back together on the strength of voter fraud.

But before, during, and after Tweed, nothing set off Nast's anti-Catholicism more than the New York school question. His most notorious sally was "The American River Ganges," which appeared in *Harper's Weekly* on September 30, 1871, shortly before the city elections that shattered Tammany Hall. The drawing shows a valiant teacher with a Bible shielding his students from crocodiles coming ashore to eat them; the Vatican is pictured on a distant horizon, while a leering Tweed and his henchmen watch from the safety of a cliff. Nast's most ingenious touch was to shape the heads and jaws of the reptiles as bishops' miters. Five years later, with the politically eclipsed Tweed behind bars, the cartoonist returned to the issue with a different ravenous animal. "Wolf at the Door, Gaunt and Hungry—Don't Let Him In" from September 16, 1876, portrays a teacher and pupils trying to hold a classroom door against a wolf that has stuck its head inside; a caption urges, "No Tax Money for Schools."

Nast's moral fervor barely acknowledged humor when it came to religion—a mood underlined by his black-and-white drawings. Still, he was no lonely beacon. Keppler, another one-time Catholic who had never gotten over that experience in particular and who had developed a general contempt for clergymen as conmen, regularly devoted pages of *Puck* to Vatican bashing. In "Business Alliance," a beaming Pope Leo XIII declares, "Bless you, my children! I think we can work together

THE AMERICAN RIVER GANGES.
THE PRIESTS AND THE CHILDREN.—(See Page 911.)

nobly in America"; the remark is addressed to two cardinals and two snarling American strikers. "The Pope's Dream—A Roman Catholic America" shows a prelate sitting in the chair of the U.S. president. None of this was new to Keppler. During the brief, earlier existence of *Puck* in St. Louis, he had rarely gotten through the day without some graphic attack on Leo XIII's predecessor Pius IX for his declaration of papal infallibility.

Both Keppler and Nast had their ecumenical moments—when they attacked Mormons as much as Catholics. Keppler's "In Memoriam Brigham Young" marked the religious leader's death in 1877 with a *Puck* cartoon that depicted a dozen sobbing brides in an enormous bed over the commentary "And the Place Which Knew Him Once Shall Know Him No More." The cartoon was such a sensation that it was sold as a separate broadside for more than two years and rescued *Puck* from grave financial problems. More gloomily, Nast's "Religious Liberty Is Guaranteed" warned that Mormons posed as much of a threat to Protestant America as the Catholics did. With the latter back as a crocodile and the Mormons symbolized by an aggressive turtle, the reptiles are shown slithering over the dome of the Capitol; the legend asks whether "we can allow foreign reptiles to crawl all over U S?" (Of all the nineteenth-century religions in America with more than a hundred followers, the Church of Jesus Christ of Latter-Day Saints was the most indigenous, the least vulnerable to being called "foreign." But it *was* based west of the Hudson River.)

Sexual stereotypes were readily available through the suffragette movement, especially in the 1890s. One hotbed of derision was *Life,* a weekly launched in January 1883 by John Ames Mitchell as a competitor to *Puck* and *Judge.* Regarded by some as the forerunner to *The New Yorker, Life* (which had no relation to the pictorial weekly published by Henry Luce in the twentieth century) became initially identified with women through the drawings of Charles Dana Gibson and his so-called Gibson Girls. Promoting the image of Gibson's well-bred, patrician young lady, however, did not leave all that much room for women who were demanding voting rights. A typical *Life* cartoon on the subject was William A. Walker's "New Navy" of April 16, 1896, in which fat, bloomered women are depicted as having taken over the military service. The usual subtheme for such portrayals, in *Life* and elsewhere, was that once summed up by an anonymous writer as "a woman looking for female rights is also looking for female charms." Those who weren't lesbians were just ugly battleaxes.

Among the derogated ethnic groups, late-century cartoonists seemed to labor most over the Jews, at least over those in the first immigrant waves from the same Central European places as many of the artists themselves. Even at their most misshapen, they were usually presented as physicians, lawyers, or some other kind of professional. Whether that depiction triggered more uneasiness by presenting Jews as a social threat or occasioned more casual passions, cartoonists were seldom able to disparage their one-time countrymen without retreating to a Currier & Ives wordiness for explaining a supposed joke. An untitled Eugene Zimmerman drawing from the December 12, 1892, issue of *Judge* goes back and forth in dialogue between a husband and wife to deliver the punchline that their son has been killed but the father has the consolation that he will be able to sue the railroad that killed him. In "A Great Opportunity" from *Puck* on March 6, 1895, Keppler has a Jew hearing that a neighbor has been diagnosed with an "enlargement of der heart" and sending his son to the man to borrow two hundred while the getting is good. Frank Beard's "A Young Financier" from *Judge* on May 12, 1894, features another father-son conversation in which the son proves his mettle by buying paper flowers for his sister's wedding so they can be used again when his grandfather dies.

With or without a short story incorporated into the panel, the running theme of the anti-Semitic cartoons was money—making it, saving it, committing arson and fraud to get more. This was nothing new to the 1880s and 1890s. In 1861, Nast pursued the theme to the extent of misrepresenting his hero Lincoln as an anti-Semite. In the August 19 edition of the *Illustrated News,* in "John Bull and the American Loan," he has Lincoln explicitly addressing a big-nosed moneylender as Shylock and parroting the bigoted canard about Jews running England. (Actually, Lincoln was the first president to crack down on anti-Semitism in the army.) Toward the end of the century, the money theme was gradually transferred to the second-wave immigrants from eastern parts of Europe, but on a lower social scale. The German Jew thought about nothing but money from within his store or medical studio; the Russian Jew exhibited the same single-mindedness while peddling cheap goods on the street.

If Jews were urban creatures looking for money, blacks were rural types habitually devising schemes to enjoy the sweet life. Their greatest preoccupations were stealing watermelons from patches and chickens from coops. An early publication obsessed with this theme was the first version of *Vanity Fair*, published between 1859 and 1863 by Charles Browne under his pen name Artemus Ward; for the alleged humorist Ward, only Lincoln deserved more contempt than blacks. The *Vanity Fair* outlook was an integral part of a racist propaganda campaign whose graphics were eventually labeled "scartoons." The work of southerners or northern Democrats, the scartoons were aimed at scaring the country away from antislavery measures through warnings that blacks would use Lincoln and abolitionist spokesmen to eventually gain power.

For his part, Nast embraced Lincoln's Emancipation Proclamation (as in "Doctor Lincoln's New Elixir of Life" for the *Illustrated News* on April 12, 1862), making for a more forbidding kind of paternalism toward African Americans. Back in the gutter was Syd Griffin's "Between Two Loves" from the September 30, 1893, edition of *Judge*; it centered around a raggedy man so encumbered by two enormous watermelons that he doesn't know what to do about the plump chicken staring at him.

BETWEEN TWO LOVES.
"Kin any one tell a po' culled man what to do in a case like dis?"

The prize for social subtlety, however, went to an unsigned cartoon in the same magazine on September 17, 1892. "Evolution of the Watermelon" shows a black face transforming itself through four figures into a watermelon.

The anti-Catholic bias against the Irish didn't need further incentives, but it got them anyway. First came New York's Orange riots between Irish Catholics and Irish Protestants in 1870 and 1871 that left seventy-five dead. Then there was the influence of John Tenniel and other British cartoonists on their American counterparts. When the Church and the bottle weren't attracting the contempt of the New York–based periodicals, the

Fenian movement's aim of gaining independence from England was. The issue gained extra heat after Irish radical Jeremiah O'Donovan Rossa was deported to New York in 1871 and began raising funds in the city on behalf of Home Rule for Ireland. A Frederick Opper drawing in *Puck* on March 7, 1883, entitled "The Irish Leeches and Their Victim," pictured an Irishman being pecked to death by diminutive creatures labeled "Peter's Pence," "Fenian Fund," "Home Rule Fund," and "Irish Catholic Banks." On February 6, 1884, Opper returned to the fray with "The Sooner the Better," showing an Irish cook rejecting the fund solicitations of an O'Donovan Rossa kind of Fenian, telling him, "Help Ireland, is it? Begorra, the best way to help Ireland wud be for you an' the likes of ye to *die* for Ireland." The cartoonist who later went on to a lucrative career drawing the comic strip "Happy Hooligan" pictures the Irishman in both pieces as a caveman in clothes—extremely reminiscent of the British illustrator Thomas Rowlandson.

The vilest treatment, however, was reserved for Native Americans, where publications like *Puck* and *Judge* considered even genocide a funny topic. One unsigned *Judge* centerfold on May 12, 1883, entitled "The Solution of a Knotty Problem," proposed shipping "indians" to Mexico on navy ships that—it was hoped—would be lost at sea. "Decidedly the two most useless, most expensive and most dangerous entities with which the country has to deal," a commentary asserted, "are the indians and its navy. If they could be made to destroy each other mutually, we would have taken a long step toward the millennium."[31] On January 17, 1891, the same magazine returned to the theme in the immediate aftermath of the Wounded Knee massacre by suggesting that the "Indian Question" might be resolved by annihilating the tribes through such (supposedly amusing) means as giving them free opium and liquor or establishing home-rule reservations for the Irish right next to standing villages.

Apparent embarrassment has prompted some historians to omit reproductions of such egregious stereotypes from their books (inevitably increasing curiosity about works otherwise elaborately described). Other researchers have excused the periodicals of the time for printing them on the grounds that the editors weren't so much racist as stressed by production deadlines. To buttress this contention, they have pointed to drawings in which *Puck*, *Judge*, and Nast in *Harper's Weekly* seemed to demonstrate sympathy for minorities, most notably Chinese and Japanese immigrants. Certainly, Nast never confused the Chinese for Catholics. In such drawings as "Every Dog Has His Day" in February 1879, "E Pluribus Unum (Except the Chinese)" in April 1882, and "Justice for the Chinese" in March 1886, he denounced the casual brutalities inflicted on the Asian immigrants, and this in the face of *Harper's Weekly* editorials demanding tighter restrictions against people from the Far East because while "the European easily blends with the American, . . . the Asiatic remains an absolute alien."[32]

According to apologists for the stereotypes, though, the real problem wasn't any deep prejudice on the part of the magazines but rather their last-minute habit of buying demeaning filler cartoons from subcontractors when it became obvious that a given issue was going to have too much white space. These arguments would stand up to more scrutiny if Asians hadn't been the most relentlessly infantilized of all immigrant groups in the period, if the Chinese in particular hadn't been concentrated in California three thousand miles away from *Puck, Judge,* and the other leading weeklies, and if the deadline defense could also be applied to the publisher who, faced with too much white space on an Alcoholics Anonymous bulletin, paid a subcontractor for pictures of his favorite bars.

6. Influence

The idea of a television news anchor influencing national attitudes about a foreign war or a weekly sitcom ridiculing a doltish politician back to private life seems quaint in the twenty-first century. But President Lyndon Johnson believed it about Walter Cronkite during the Vietnam hostilities and Vice-President Dan Quayle believed it about the CBS show "Murphy Brown" in the early 1990s. In the nineteenth century, there were plenty of political leaders who credited or blamed cartoonists for their political ups and downs. Sometimes they were being gracious, at other times they were sulking, and at still other times they were reaching for any explanation at all for what had happened to them. One way or the other, the employers of the cartoonists were happy to hear they had made a difference—even when the evidence wasn't always there that they had. It was good for business.

Both Lincoln and Grant explicitly acknowledged the support they received from Nast's work in *Harper's Weekly,* the first mass weekly largely sold through subscription on a national level. For Lincoln, the cartoonist was "our best recruiting sergeant" for the drawings he did from the battlefields of the Civil War.[33] Probably just as important for the White House occupant was "Compromise with the South," a September 3, 1864, Nast cartoon that bitterly mocked the peace platform of the Democrats in their election-year attempt to dump Lincoln for George McClellan. The cartoon shows a crippled veteran having to shake hands with a cocky Confederate officer over the grave of Union soldiers killed during what is described as a "useless war." The Republicans reproduced the scornful cartoon by the millions as part of their campaign literature, and it was credited with helping to get Lincoln reelected. If this was true, it had substantial help from McClellan's transparent queasiness about playing the dove after having been the commander of the Union Army, as well as from the implacable aversion of American voters to ousting a president during a war.

Four years later, in 1868, Grant was quoted as saying that his triumph over Democrat Horatio Seymour was due to "the sword of Sheridan and the pencil of Thomas Nast."[34] He had even more reason to be grateful for the cartoonist's help subsequently—first because of Nast's steadfast refusal to acknowledge the numerous corruption scandals during the general's White House tenure and then with his successful reelection bid over Horace Greeley in 1872. Nast's scorn for Greeley was such that the fabled New York *Tribune* editor once cracked that he didn't know if he were running for the presidency or the penitentiary. The hostility became so marked that Democrat Frank Leslie brought British cartoonist Matt Morgan over from London in an attempt to counter Nast's illustrations through his own *Illustrated News.* The only thing Morgan succeeded in doing was escalating the savagery between the two publications; beyond that, he was no match for Nast's moralistic ferocity against the liberal Republican–Democratic candidate. Even the fact that Greeley was seriously ailing and his wife had recently died didn't stop Nast from playing with death themes. One November 6, 1872, illustration, "We Are on the Home Stretch," showed Greeley's corpse being carried away on a stretcher; to double the dose, Nast framed the picture against the front page of Greeley's own *Tribune*. Graphics of the kind left the cartoonist open to bitter recriminations when Greeley, broken both physically and mentally, died only three weeks after losing the election to Grant. The editor's running mate fared better only insofar as he didn't go to an early grave. Reportedly because he couldn't come up with a fitting caricature for Benjamin Gratz Brown, Nast reduced the Missouri governor to a clothing tag on Greeley's suit. That was about as witty as things got.

But if there was one election in the nineteenth century that gave cartoonists visions of being power brokers, it was the 1884 contest between the Democratic

"WE ARE ON THE HOME STRETCH."—*New York Tribune, October 9, 1872.*

governor of New York, Grover Cleveland, and Maine Republican James G. Blaine—referred to by one historian as "the highwater line . . . of purely personal abuse in [American] comic art."[35] As he had done with Lincoln's successor, Andrew Johnson, Nast broke with his Republican loyalties, asserting that Blaine, a former senator with a major graft scandal on his resume, didn't represent the party's liberal values; along with a host of other New York Republican luminaries, he joined the "mugwump" (i.e., sitting on the fence with their mugs on one side, their wumps on the other) defection to Cleveland. It didn't hurt that the cartoonist's ferocious anti-Catholic sentiments were stirred by Blaine's attempt to win over Irish Democrats (the candidate was already suspect for having a Catholic mother) or that Cleveland shared his animus toward Tammany Hall. Nast's backing of the Democratic governor delighted rivals, who wasted little time making this the theme of various caricature portrayals of the cartoonist. But it was Blaine who ended up with the more serious wounds to lick.

The first big attack came from Keppler's *Puck* on June 4, 1884, with Bernhard Gillam portraying the Republican candidate as the Tattooed Man in "Phryne before the Chicago Tribunal." The color illustration was a takeoff on a French painting by Jean-Leon Gerome that had caused a stir in Paris some years earlier. Its subject was the way the Greek orator Hyperides, defending the prostitute Phryne against charges of profanity for posing for a statue of Aphrodite, got her acquitted by throwing off her robe and daring her judges to dispute her naked loveliness. In the role of Phryne, a decidedly unaesthetic-looking Blaine, his body covered with tattooed references to the various scandals of his past, has to hide his face in shame before his judges. A contemporary observer cited by Hess and Kaplan said the illustration made him "feel a certain irresistible thrill of loathing."[36] The candidate had to be talked out of suing *Puck* for libel and obscenity when the Gillam cartoon proved as much of a sensation in the United States as the Gerome original had been in France. Keppler didn't have to be talked out of—or into—anything. His penchant for tagging politicians with a fixed image, particularly during election contests, led him to depict Blaine relentlessly as the Tattooed Man for the rest of the campaign.

That wasn't the worst of it for the Republican. On October 30, 1884, five days before the election, the New York *World* came out with an enormous front-page cartoon entitled "The Royal Feast of Belshazzar Blaine and the Money Kings," referring to a banquet at the posh Delmonico's on Park Avenue at which the candidate had been wined and dined by the city's power elite. Drawn by Walt McDougall with an assist from portraitist Valerian Gribayedoff, the drawing showed Jay Gould, Jacob Astor, Andrew Carnegie, and other plutocrats digging into such dishes as Lobby Pudding, Monopoly Soup, and Navy Contracts while an impoverished family tries futilely to get their attention for a handout. The piece had ended up at the *World* only because McDougall had been passing the newspaper's offices after having it rejected by Keppler at *Puck* (apparently because the weekly had run a similarly themed cartoon in June). The submission on spec was the start of something loud. As the Republicans had done twenty years earlier with Nast's "Compromise with the South," the Democrats went into mass production on the McDougall cartoon, even making billboards from it. Blaine ended up losing New York by only one

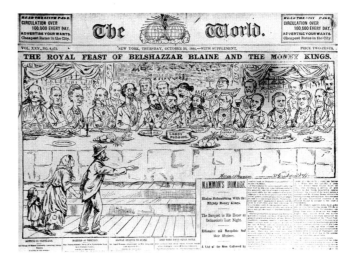

thousand one hundred votes. Since he would have won the election if he had carried the state, many attributed the first Democratic victory since James Buchanan in 1856 to "Balshazzar Blaine" and the Tattooed Man.

But their new prominence notwithstanding, the Blaine affair still amounted to leaky proof that political cartoons were ready to weigh decisively on national elections. The only point beyond dispute is that the *World* illustration persuaded daily newspaper publishers once and for all that cartoons shouldn't be left to *Puck, Harper's Weekly*, and other weekly periodicals. Over the next decade, graphic commentary would add to the appeal of the newspaper-buying habit. By the same token, the daily press's greater interest in the genre was a hard body blow to the magazines. Keppler proved to be the first victim when Gillam, a life-long Republican who didn't sleep too well after helping to push Blaine off the ledge with the Tattooed Man, left *Puck* to resuscitate its fading competitor *Judge*. More generally, not only did the periodicals have to watch their most gifted cartoonists waltz away for the bigger contracts and greater visibility offered by the daily press, but they gradually lost their standing as hubs for political controversy. The revival of Gillam's Republican-oriented *Judge* and the arrival of Mitchell's *Life* temporarily heated up the weekly market in terms of both circulation combat and political polemics, but all were soon in a struggle for survival.

The overall political significance of the anti-Blaine cartoons was much muddier than the ramifications within the media world. For one thing, New York's critical role in determining the election outcome didn't so much provide a continental stage for the Tattooed Man as it illuminated the adage that all politics are local. While it has been a commonplace to indicate the 1884 vote as the centerpiece for an unprecedented boom period for cartoons, magazine artists indisputably showed far more clout when they were having a say about municipal questions than when they were contributing to national debates, and given the anomalous importance of New York for the election, Blaine had marked local properties. For his part, the candidate had done everything possible to sabotage what had once been a healthy lead over Cleveland in the state. After alienating his big-money Republican base by fishing for votes among Irish immigrants, he had promptly angered the Irish by seeming to endorse a widely repeated flippancy by a Republican preacher that linked the immigrants to "rum, Romanism, and rebellion." In short, long before the *World* published its version of the Delmonico's banquet, numerous Republicans had made it clear they would be no-shows, and very few Democrats would have been surprised by McDougall's menu.

The next signal event in political cartooning also said more about the craft's ability to startle, nag, and amuse than about its power to alter thinking in the voting booth. By 1896, William Randolph Hearst had moved from the San Francisco *Examiner* to New York to buy the floundering *Journal* and establish it as the chief competitor to Pulitzer's *World*. Moving with him was Homer Davenport, the first major daily newspaper cartoonist. In his support of Democrat William Jennings Bryan against William McKinley, Hearst was initially stymied by the Republican candidate's scandal-free record. But then he and Davenport decided to concentrate their attack on McKinley's chief strategist, Mark Hanna, a political manipulator for whom the country was divided into two parts—millionaire industrialists and everybody else. Typical of the cartoons was "A Man of Mark" on August 4, 1896; one of a series with the same caption, it showed Hanna's big hand coming out of a jacket cuff covered with dollar signs dangling McKinley at the end of a chain. Another on September 3, "Wall Street Wishes a New Guardian of the Treasury," depicts George Washington's statue on Wall Street being replaced with one of Hanna. As always, the walrus-shaped Republican is represented as bulging out of a waistcoat with a dollar-sign pattern. (It wasn't subtle, but, notwithstanding treatises by historians insisting on the rarefied wit of the best cartoons, very little of it ever has been.)

The Hanna cartoons about greed, greed, and more greed not only became the talk of the campaign but also wore on their protagonist. On one occasion, Hanna was reported to have broken down in tears after seeing a Davenport illustration, complaining that it "hurts to be held up to the gaze of the world as a murderer of women and children."[37] After the election, in an apparently more philosophical mood, he told Davenport, "I admire your execution but damn your conception."[38] That—and increased circulation for the *Journal*—was as good as it got for Hearst. Not only was McKinley elected, but he demolished Bryan in New York and in most of the northeast states and New England. When the two squared off again in 1900, the outcome was the same.

That wasn't enough for the victors. Between the two elections, there was enough of a perception in some back rooms that the cartoons *did* hurt that politicians resorted to the law to try to crack down on them. With Hearst and Davenport clearly in mind, New York Republican leader Thomas Platt got the retaliations going in 1897 with a bill that would have made cartoonists and their employers far more vulnerable to libel. Davenport's response was an April 22 cartoon—"No Honest Man Need Fear Cartoons"—that linked "Boss" Platt to "Boss" Tweed. A few days later, after the bill had been quashed, the cartoonist depicted himself as laughing and Platt and Tweed as crying in "There Are Some Who Laugh and Others Who Weep." The reprisals didn't sputter out so quickly in California and Pennsylvania. In 1899 in California, where the Southern Pacific Railroad controlled both party machines and the legislative process was itself a cartoon, there was little suspense leading up to the state assembly's passage of a bill that made it a crime to publish any caricature without the consent of the subject. Unfortunately for the Southern Pacific Railroad and its political minions, that was the last time anybody took the bill seriously. But for comic absurdity, California paled next to Pennsylvania.

In January 1903, Samuel Pennypacker took office as Pennsylvania governor with a vow to stamp out what he called "worthless" newspapers that practiced "the kind of slander which is closely akin to treason." The threat was directed most immediately at the Philadelphia *North American* and its cartoonists Charles Nelan and McDougall of "Balshazzar Blaine" fame. Nelan's favorite vision of Pennypacker had been as a parrot that could only mouth words given to him by state Republican boss, Matthew Quay. A week after the inauguration, the Republicans introduced a bill that made it a crime to publish any cartoon "portraying, describing, or representing any person . . . in the form or likeness of a beast, bird, fish, insect, or other unhuman animal."[39] McDougall's reply was to portray Pennypacker as a stein of beer and Quay as a dying oak, along with the warning that the legislation should have "included more than the animal kingdom alone, for we have an ample field in the vegetable, if not even the mineral field. . . . What chances of caricature lie in the tomato, the string bean, the cucumber, the onion, and the leek cannot be guessed."[40] When Pennypacker signed the bill anyway, he was deluged with hundreds of newspaper editorials from around the country describing the measure as, in the words of the *New York Times*, "the most reactionary that has passed any legislature in recent years."[41] It took a few years for the law to be taken off the books, but there were no successful prosecutions under it.

The fiascos in New York, California, and Pennsylvania didn't prevent a couple of other states (Alabama and Indiana) from also seeking legal measures to muzzle cartoonists—or the artists from gloating about their ultimate victories. But what did that say about the practical political influence of cartoons? Much less than the cartoonists and their employers wanted to admit. The legislative maneuvers were the work of parties or individuals that had secured or maintained power despite the antagonism of the targeted cartoonists. That might have made the politicians personally vindictive and institutionally repressive, but it didn't make them electoral losers. If there was any evidence at all for cartoon impact on voters around the turn of the century, it had to be sought in the sheer profusion of illustrations in the daily press and, more important, in the relative drawing power of the papers printing them. Hearst and Davenport's anti-Hanna strategy might have marked a brilliant moment in cartoon history, might have created the kind of editorial noise no politician would have welcomed, but far more anti-Bryan dailies with their hired pens made sure that was only a footnote to American electoral annals. As its leading practitioners have said repeatedly, editorial cartooning has never been just about the art.

Another example of the questionable national political influence of cartooning in the period came from its attacks on business monopolies. As historians Allan Nevins and Henry Steele Commager have described the life of an average city dweller in the 1890s,

> When he sat down to breakfast he ate bacon packaged by the beef trust, seasoned his eggs with salt made by the Michigan salt trust, sweetened his coffee with sugar refined by the American Sugar trust, lit his American Tobacco cigar with a Diamond Match Company match. Then he rode to work on a bicycle built by the bicycle trust or on a trolley car operating under a monopolistic franchise and running on steel rails made by United States Steel.[42]

Practically on a daily basis, cartoonists across the political spectrum designed negative trust figures, usually

THE BOSSES OF THE SENATE.

along the lines of a bloated, demonic Shrek, as in Opper's "Alphabet of Joyous Trusts." Another illustration of the same kind was Keppler's "Bosses of the Senate" in the January 23, 1889, issue of *Puck*, in which monstrous figures in high hats and vests stand behind the Senate floor to make sure their interests are being promoted; across their ample moneybag bellies are such phrases as "Steel Beam Trust," "Copper Trust," and "Sugar Trust." More biblical was Davenport, who, enthused by a statue he saw in Venice, imagined the monopolist as a brutal Samson, as in "The Head of the Procession Coming out of Wall Street," a drawing for the New York *Journal and Advertiser* on November 4, 1900. But for all their regularity, such illustrations proved so generic as to be evasive. When it came to dealing with the real consequences of the trusts (for example, thirty-seven thousand labor strikes between 1881 and 1905), cartoonists either ran out of ink or, as in Keppler's case, accused workers of being a more immediate problem for having instigated clashes with police or factory goons. The chief exceptions came when Big Capital bosses figured in another agenda, such as in the June 16, 1900, *Journal* cartoon "Mr. Hanna's Stand on the Labor Question," in which the Republican strategist is shown standing on the skull of Labor within the paper's campaign against McKinley's reelection. In the meantime, the monopolists shrugged off what soon became innocuous cartoon attention and continued to thrive.

So did cartoonists—but in new ways.

7. Expansions

As the nineteenth century drew to a close, Hearst and Pulitzer had a lot more on their minds—and on their presses—than McKinley and Bryan. Foremost were comic strips, advertisers, and Spain.

In 1896, the single most popular feature of the *World* was Richard Outcault's colored Sunday panel "Hogan's Alley," which centered around the character of the Yellow Dugan Kid, a toothless, hairless Irish urchin in a yellow nightshirt who shared his epiphanies from the streets and backyards of New York's working neighborhoods. If there was a political tinge to the Kid's wanderings (the May 15, 1896, drawing "The War Scare Reaches Hogan's Alley," for example, depicted a line of ragamuffins with signs proclaiming "Down wit Ingland" and "Down wit Spane"), there was far more street smart folksiness and a prevailing feel of kids winking at any and all adult exertions. In October, Hearst, who had already stolen readers from Pulitzer by offering a separate sports section every day, lured Outcault away from his rival. An enraged Pulitzer sued, but managed only half a victory in court—the *World* could continue running

"Hogan's Alley" with artist George Luks, but Outcault had the right to draw his copyrighted Yellow Kid for the *Journal.* Considered the first true comic strip, the Yellow Kid proved even more popular for Hearst than for Pulitzer. The fact that Outcault's creation appeared in both the *World* and the *Journal* helped consolidate its paternity of the term "yellow journalism" for the reporting approaches of the two sensationalist dailies (though rival New York *Press* editor Ervin Wardman was also known to have previously criticized Hearst and Pulitzer for their "yell kid journalism").

A year after bringing in Outcault, Hearst hired Rudolph Dirks to draw "The Katzenjammer Kids" for the *Journal's* Sunday supplement, the eight-page color section known as *The American Humorist.* The first strip to employ a series of panels to tell a story, "The Katzenjammer Kids" featured the brats Hans and Fritz, who were forever playing pranks on their mother, a vaguely defined sea captain, and an even more nebulous inspector —all of them speaking in heavy German accents. (When Hearst tried to prevent Dirks from taking a leave of absence shortly before World War I, he had the tables turned on him from the Yellow Kid conflict: Dirks took his creation to Pulitzer while the *Journal* continued the series with a substitute artist.)

In 1900, Hearst also signed Frederick Opper away from *Puck.* Initially employed on an anti-McKinley propaganda series called "Willie and His Poppa" for that year's presidential elections, Opper, who had specialized in anti-Irish cartoons, soon undertook the vapid "Happy Hooligan" strip. Accompanied by his brothers Gloomy Gus and Lord Montmorency and his dog Flip, Hooligan, in a tiny tin hat and otherwise attired like a

hobo, went from one minor mischief to another. The strip's most enduring legacy turned out to be the impetus it gave mass merchandising; the Hooligan figure was sold as everything from dolls to a motion picture series. On November 15, 1907, the same Hearst's San Francisco *Examiner* premiered the first daily strip—Bud Fisher's "A. Mutt" (later to be known as "Mutt and Jeff"). While taking shots at politics, it was initially popular as a sports page feature for Mutt's racing tips.

Hearst's aggressive signing of anybody who could help consolidate the comic strip as a signature of his press empire led to what was arguably the single funniest cartoon in the early twentieth century. When the publisher started making moves on the Democratic presidential nomination in 1904, *Puck* cartoonist J. S. Pughe responded with a June illustration called "If" that imagined what an inaugural White House dinner with Hearst presiding might look like. What it would look like, according to Pughe, would be a drunken Hearst raising his glass to his guests—the Katzenjammers, Happy Hooligan, Gloomy Gus, and all his other comic strip characters.

The rapid popularity of the "funnies" was not lost on cartoonists, who didn't have to have their arms twisted to switch to bigger pay envelopes. The comic strip creators even helped raise editorial cartoonists to a new level of celebrity. In the early years of the twentieth century, they cut ribbons, served as grand marshals of parades, and drew prestigious speaking assignments. The month that went by without some magazine profile of an Opper or Davenport wasn't on the calendar. An otherwise stodgy periodical like Boston's *Arena* not only slipped an appreciation of a cartoonist between an academic piece on Nathaniel Hawthorne and a vapid address on the "Present Status of Cooperation in Great Britain" but also accompanied it with four pages of cartoons. For *Arena* editor B. O. Flower, who personally wrote the profiles for his periodical, cartoonists stood tall "among those who place principle above policy." "Few indeed are they to whom the vision of the ideal is sufficiently compelling to make them so indifferent to personal ease, fame, fortune, and life itself that they unhesitatingly place the cause of justice and human rights . . . above every consideration of self," Flower blustered. "Few are great enough to make the choice that lifts the soul to the peerage of the immortals who have helped the world onward."[43]

Such florid tributes came even as the traditional one-panel cartoonists themselves were getting decidedly simpler in their language, seeking imagery in ascending popular culture. Previously commonplace metaphors from mythological, classical, and Shakespearian sources gradually ceded the field to references from the sports world, the circus, minstrelsy, and other mass entertainments and pastimes. It was not an overnight change. On the one hand, for instance, *Puck* was markedly more responsive to the new social stirrings than was Nast, who continued to layer his commentaries in allusions to Shakespeare, Dante, and the other lights of proper education. But not even Keppler was totally captive to the new cultural assumptions, frequently filling *Puck* with what today would be considered even more esoteric references than Nast was producing at *Harper's Weekly*. As Fischer has observed, this did not cost him commercially. "Clearly, cartoons predicated upon an immediate, widespread recognition of the works of Millet and

Zamacois, the legends of Canute and Gambrinus, the evil of Moloch and the Minotaur, and the travails of Tantalus, the Daniades, and the gallant Rizpah either mirrored faithfully the prevailing cultural heritage of the day or failed as cartoon art through elitist obscurity."[44] At least until the daily newspapers hit their stride in the 1890s, it was very much the former.

But Canute's days were numbered. The additions of the Yellow Kid and Happy Hooligan to the *Journal* pleased a lot more people than were up on their Danish kings. Readers liked following the wanderings of the characters the way soap opera fans of another generation would follow the agonies of theirs. By the end of the century, Hearst was selling as many as 1.5 million papers a day in New York City (Pulitzer about one million) and was able to supply sister dailies around the country with a broad variety of syndicate material. And then there were the advertisers, who had come to take up half the *Journal* (and the *World*) with type and visuals. For the advertising industry, a Yellow Kid threatened none of the estrangement of potential customers that a Mark Hanna as rendered by Davenport did, and it had less and less hesitation about conveying that point of view to all the Hearsts. Even publishers who made thrilling speeches about the integrity of their editorial policies had come to rely on advertising income enough to play down, if not eliminate completely, the practice of sticking political cartoons on the front page.

But there was one topic no circulation-hungry publisher of the era would have ever agreed to take off the front page—Spanish control over Cuba. Legends to the contrary, the so-called Ten-Week War of 1898 was not the personal concoction of Hearst and Pulitzer. Numer-ous other newspapers and political interests, notably in the Midwest and West, had been pressing Washington since the end of the Mexican War in 1848 to support a nationalist Cuban revolt on the Caribbean island—either to set the stage for a colonial takeover or at the very least to regenerate American investments there. In his pre-*Puck* days, in 1872, Keppler had delighted in taunting Grant for not declaring war on Spain. Even within New York, the *Herald* and *Sun* were as jingoist as the *Journal*, and all of them found a willing ally in the Associated Press. For another New York daily, the *Record*, a war with Spain over Cuba "would be a holiday campaign and nothing more."[45] Although McKinley showed little taste for hostilities, his Navy Department, especially Assistant Secretary Theodore Roosevelt, was itching to test the expansionist sea power theories of Captain Alfred Thayer Mahan against the Spanish. Nevertheless, in spite of all these other pressures, the drive to war would ultimately be symbolized by an alleged exchange between Hearst and *Journal* cartoonist Frederic Remington. According to this tale, Remington got restless during an 1897 visit to Cuba and wired for permission to return home. "Please remain," was Hearst's reputed response. "You furnish the pictures and I'll furnish the war."[46]

Hearst always disputed having said such a thing, but what he couldn't deny were the fiction-blessed cartoons, stories, and photos he contributed to the war fever. The most infamous of the illustrations, on February 10, 1897, joined Remington and photography for "Spaniards Search Women on American Steamers," depicting a naked woman surrounded by swarthy officials who are going through the clothes they have taken off her. The story behind the picture came from *Journal* correspondent Richard Harding Davis, who, sailing home from Cuba, met Clemencia Arango, one of three women being deported from the island for suspected guerilla sympathies; according to Arango, she and her friends had been stripsearched twice before being allowed to leave. Although Davis's own report did not specify the sex of the guards who had done the searches, Remington (and Hearst) decided that men, rather than the matrons who had actually conducted them, made for more inflammatory copy. When Arango complained to Pulitzer about how her story had been twisted by the *Journal*, the *World* couldn't chortle enough at Davis, Remington, and Hearst. But though up to then the Pulitzer paper had never been as jingoistic as some of its rivals, it too fell to interventionist fever, carrying daily lurid fictions from Havana about "blood on the roadsides, blood in the fields, blood on the doorsteps, blood, blood, blood."[47]

As much as cartoonists had to say about Cuba, they had relatively little to say about the slaughters that engulfed the Philippines a year after the Spanish were driven from Manila. With McKinley claiming encouragement from God to Christianize the Filipinos,[48] the United States mercilessly squashed a local independence movement in a naked colonizing campaign. The aggression drew resistance from the Anti-Imperialist League of Bryan, Mark Twain, Jane Addams, and other notables, but the estimated deaths of some six hundred thousand Filipinos on the island of Luzon alone during hostilities and related reprisals among the natives produced only small pockets of opposition in major American newspapers. One of the few fervent dissenters was

William A. Walker of *Life*, whose drawings portrayed Uncle Sam as being bent on the same imperialist course as John Bull in Sudan and India. Otherwise, there was at best a glib admission that the Filipinos hadn't been looking for all that salvation McKinley had brought them. An April 9, 1899, cartoon in Utica's *Saturday Globe* by William Carson, for example, has Uncle Sam wrestling with guerilla leader Emilio Aguinaldo in a swamp. The caption reads "A Bigger Job Than He Thought For" and cites Sam saying, "Behave you fool! Durn Me If I Ain't Most Sorry I Undertook to Rescue You."

The same condescension plus some timely racism permeated the main graphic theme to emerge from the Philippines brutality—the question of what the United States would do with all the territories it had grabbed from the Spanish and the local populations. Thus, the Minneapolis *Tribune* printed one cartoon showing McKinley with his hand around the neck of a

A BIGGER JOB THAN HE THOUGHT FOR.
UNCLE SAM—Behave, You Fool! Durn Me, If I Ain't Most Sorry I Undertook to Rescue You.

UNCLE SAM'S NEW CLASS IN THE ART OF SELF-GOVERNMENT.

black child at the edge of a precipice and being watched by a humanized globe; the caption was "The Eyes of the World Are upon Him." The implication was that to give the child—depicted as a cowering black savage—back to the Spanish would have been the same as tossing him off the cliff. Another symptomatic motif was Uncle Sam in the role of a teacher having to deal with unruly blacks, Latins, and Hawaiians in the back of the classroom while whites sit obediently at their desks.

Along with comic strips and their own celebrity, cartoonists in the early twentieth century had an ideal professional distraction in Roosevelt. Even before succeeding the assassinated McKinley in 1901, Teddy had kept cartoonists busy with his tours as New York City

police commissioner, as assistant secretary for the navy, as a Rough Rider, and as governor of New York. He was, in fact, so unavoidable from so many points of view that he became a staple for anyone with a pen in his hand. Physically, Roosevelt's teeth, mustache, and glasses (or pince-nez) were naturals. Politically, his swipes at the trusts, approximate as many of them might have been, gave illustrators something to draw in that area besides their Shreks. Then there was his penchant for phrase making ("my hat's in the ring," "muckrakers," "I feel like a bull moose," "speak softly and carry a big stick," etc.) that eliminated a lot of tedious homework. If it wasn't all Roosevelt all the time for cartoonists, it was close to it, and with innumerably more outlets than during the similar absorption with Lincoln.

Roosevelt's ideological veerings left and right produced a zigzag course for cartoonists, as well. The same cartoonist who portrayed him acidly on Tuesday for fomenting trouble in Panama to ensure the building of a canal depicted him sympathetically on Wednesday for defending the right of Japanese children to attend California schools. One of the few who didn't blow with Teddy's winds was Robert Minor of the St. Louis *Post-Dispatch.* A socialist by conviction, the Texas-born Minor began his career with the *Post-Dispatch* by going to the morgue every morning and sketching the corpses so the pictures could accompany the usually grisly details of St. Louis's latest deaths. He went from this $18-a-week assignment to a standing as the country's highest-paid cartoonist within seven years.

That Minor managed his professional ascent for a major daily with his declared politics reflected both his talent and the accepted position of Eugene Debs's

Socialist Party at the time (there were more than three hundred socialist periodicals in the country in 1912–13). In fact, the cartoonist had more trouble with his drawing technique than with his beliefs. Eschewing the usual pen and ink, he opted for an unsubtle grease crayon on textured paper, insisting that his subjects (primarily workers and women) weren't delicate so his instruments shouldn't have been, either. He won his point, but only after long hours in the pressroom working out objections from pressmen who said his crayon style couldn't be printed. Because the technique did not permit much detail, it made for a relatively simple look and, through Rollin Kirby, Boardman Robinson, and Daniel R. Fitzpatrick, would gradually come to dominate cartooning for more than fifty years.

By 1911, Minor had become such a desirable prize that the *World* offered him a perks-laden contract to leave St. Louis for New York. But intent on going to Europe for a year, he wanted still more, so he worked out an arrangement under which the paper practically underwrote his sojourn on the Continent. The Minor who returned to the United States in 1913 was no longer a socialist but an anarchist bent on denouncing Europe's drift toward war as a scheme by bankers and industrialists for personal profit. (Still later, he would become the most orthodox of communists, running as a party candidate for governor, mayor, and senator.) At first, his anarchist outlook proved no problem for the *World*, which was anti-interventionist, if for entirely different reasons. But when the paper came around to the pro-war stance of the Woodrow Wilson administration and Minor refused to get in line, he was shown the door. In his case at least, it didn't have bars on it.

8. Prohibitions

No sooner had Charles Philipon launched his magazine *Le Charivari* in France in 1831 than he and his chief cartoonist Honoré Daumier were thrown into prison for six months for insulting the king. In the United States, prior to World War I, attempts to suppress political cartoons were sporadic and regional, and frequently farcical. The most blatant try at a payoff, at least according to Nast, had been a Tweed offer of $100,000 if the cartoonist went to Europe to "study art" instead of attacking him. Nast toyed with a Tammany Hall emissary until he had the would-be bribe up to $500,000, and then finally replied that he wasn't interested in going abroad. Before dangling the carrot, Tweed had swung the stick by cutting off textbook sales to the city's schools by the publishers of *Harper's Weekly*, an important source of the house's income. The five states resorting to anticartoon legislation also believed in the heavy hand. But all these efforts were just exploratory jabs compared to the hammering carried out in the name of the Espionage Statute of 1917.

For most of the country, the most conspicuous effect of the World War I measure was that it gave the green light to vigilante thugs, especially those claiming membership in the American Protective League, to accost anyone at all on the street and demand proof of draft status; in the month of September 1917 in New York alone, this led to some fifty thousand males being detained. The following summer, cartoonists had a private warden of their own with the establishment of a Bureau of Cartoons within a federal propaganda department. An August 31, 1918, declaration issued through a weekly

Bulletin for Cartoonists told illustrators that "through your cartoons you can inspire in every man a keen sense of his obligations to the cause of democracy and stimulate public opinion on this vital issue [the war] as few other forces in this country can."[49]

What was stimulated was a rigid adherence to the war policies of the Wilson White House. Some cartoonists, such as Ding Darling of the Des Moines *Register*, had already been leaning that way, particularly after 128 Americans had been lost in the 1915 German U-boat sinking of the British liner *Luisitania*. But with the Espionage Act, there was little room for any other position, at least on big-circulation dailies. When illustrators weren't depicting the "Hun" committing some atrocity, they were crowing over American forces smashing him up on the battlefield or reminding German Americans where their loyalties should lie. In cities with appreciable German populations, such as Cincinnati, Milwaukee, and St. Louis, the vicious and the viciously stereotypical approached the norm. James Montgomery Flagg epitomized the regimented cheerleading with one cover of the *Bulletin for Cartoonists* that showed him forcing the Kaiser to look into a mirror to see the skull of a dead man; dispensing with false modesty, Flagg captioned the drawing "The Cartoonist Makes People See Things." Flagg, Oscar Cesare, Harold Tucker Webster (before his Caspar Milquetoast days), and scores of others also lent their skills to enlistment and Liberty Bonds posters. Another group of artists, including Wallace Morgan of the New York *Sun*, gained commissions as officers to cover their service as official army illustrators.

If any cartoonist from the pro-war ranks distinguished himself in the press, it wasn't an American at

COMMITTEE ON PUBLIC INFORMATION

GEORGE CREEL, *Chairman*
THE SECRETARY OF STATE
THE SECRETARY OF WAR
THE SECRETARY OF THE NAVY

Bureau of Cartoons Bulletin No. 20

BULLETIN FOR CARTOONISTS

OCTOBER 26, 1918

JAMES MONTGOMERY FLAGG

THE CARTOONIST MAKES PEOPLE SEE THINGS!

all, but the Dutchman Louis Raemaekers. Raemaekers should have had a foot up on journalistic objectivity in view of his country's neutrality in the European hostilities, but in fact his cartoons in Amsterdam's *De Telegraaf* were so venomous toward the Kaiser that he was arrested and tried for imperiling Holland's diplomatic stance. Although acquitted, the artist heard enough about the bounty put on his head by Berlin not to trust his Amsterdam surroundings, so he went to London, where he continued his drawing for the daily *Times* (and apparently dodged at least one assassination attempt). In September 1917, Raemaekers signed a contract with Hearst—an arrangement that provided him with a regular American audience and the publisher with a shield against threatened government action for alleged disloyalty to the national cause. This contract also gave the artist an excuse to visit the United States, where he made a grand tour that enabled everyone to see how obsessed he was by the Kaiser. But not even Raemaeker's manic personality discouraged the American public from appreciating the harrowing tragedy he incorporated into his contempt for Imperial Germany; one 1917 piece, "Kultur Has Passed Here," portrays a mother and a child, the clothes of both barely on them, lying dead on the ground. Although he used the tritest of motifs for depicting the savagery of war, cruelty, beauty, and waste all suffuse the cartoon.

The most prominent critic of American intervention on a major paper was Luther Bradley of the Chicago *Daily News.* His point of view was a mixture of isolationism and a-plague-on-both-your-houses. One of his most effective drawings, published on May 29, 1916, and entitled "The Seat of the Trouble," has a nurse looking at the teeth of a globe in the role of a bedded hospital patient and saying, "You'll have no health nor comfort till you get rid of those crowns." Otherwise, resistance was largely confined to small literary and political magazines, where socialists, anarchists, and bohemians made common pacifist cause.

The most significant of the small periodicals was the Greenwich Village monthly *The Masses,* refounded as a socialist-slanted cooperative in 1911 under the editorship of Max Eastman and the art direction of painter John Sloan after a previous stop-and-go existence as a radical publication. Its jaunty aim was to appeal "to the masses, both Socialist and non-Socialist, with entertainment, education, and the livelier kinds of propaganda."[50] Contributors over the years would include Bertrand Russell, Carl Sandburg, Upton Sinclair, Lincoln Steffens, Amy Lowell, Walter Lippmann, and even Pablo Picasso. In addition to the looming conflict in Europe, the magazine focused on such issues as working women, child labor, and trade union rights. One of its more trenchant cartoons had Anthony Comstock, the deeply troubled head of the New York City Society for the Suppression of Vice, dragging a woman into court for having given birth to a naked baby.

As the mainstream press fell into line under Washington pressures, *The Masses* increasingly served as an outlet for cartoons rejected elsewhere for political reasons. This also brought about a staff conflict that again pointed up the special nature of the editorial cartoon. When Sloan proposed that the magazine's illustrations be run without captions, a group headed by cartoonist Art Young objected that this would make it just another periodical interested in art for art's sake. "For my part," Young said, "I do not care to be connected with a publication that does not try to point the way out of a sordid materialistic world."[51] The wrangle ended with Young replacing Sloan as art editor. Among those who worked under him was Minor, whose July 1916 "Army Medical Examiner," showing a headless Hercules of a draftee as the "perfect soldier," was one of the starkest images from wartime cartooning. Another contributor was Boardman Robinson, who, like Minor with the *World*, had lost his job at the New York *Tribune* because of his views against the war.

But it was Young (described by a contemporary as a "kindhearted soldier with a machine gun") who quickly became the conscience of the magazine. A veteran freelancer who had contributed at one time or another to just about every weekly magazine and daily paper in Chicago and New York, he once returned a $100 check to *Life* magazine after deciding that he couldn't live with an anti-immigrant cartoon he had delivered for an assignment. The socialist artist made it clear where he stood on World War I with his regular depictions of Wilson as a devil or a bum and with such drawings as "Having Their Fling." In the latter, published in the September 1917 issue of *The Masses*, an editor, a capitalist, a politician, and a minister are shown cavorting behind their respective placards of "All for Democracy," "All for Honor," "All for World Peace," and "All for Jesus" while the devil

"Army Medical Examiner: 'At last a perfect soldier!'"

conducts a symphony of cannons. At the time, however, not too many people got to see "Having Their Fling."

Two months earlier, Postmaster General Albert Burleson had declared *The Masses* "unmailable" because of its alleged "obstruction of recruitment." Since magazines of the kind were heavily dependent on subscribers, the block on mailing effectively ended their distribution. Using a backup Sedition Act of 1918 to help him fill in the blanks in the original Espionage Statute, Burleson used the same weapon to crack down on an estimated seventy-five journals, most of them run by socialists with official or unofficial ties to the Debs party. When Judge Learned Hand agreed with Eastman's arguments that his civil rights had been violated, Burleson sought out a conservative Vermont judge for lodging an appeal. Between the New England court's deliberate delay and then a ruling against the editor, *The Masses* was forced out of business before the end of the year.

Burleson didn't stop there. The following spring, Eastman, Young, writer Floyd Dell, and other contributors were indicted on the obstruction charge, which carried a twenty-year prison sentence. When the first trial ended in a hung jury, Burleson insisted on yet another go-'round in January 1919, months after the end of the war. That too produced a hung jury. If nothing else, the trials gave Young a public forum for demonstrating the sense of humor that was equal to his militancy. When he wasn't interrupting the prosecutor by heckling the questions asked of witnesses, the cartoonist was napping at the defense table, inspiring one sardonic self-portrait entitled "Art Young on Trial for His Life."

Young and his colleagues on *The Masses* were luckier than others. Maurice Becker, another contributor to the magazine, drew twenty-five years at hard labor for desertion. Becker had sought nonreligious conscientious objection status, had gone to Mexico after his draft board had rejected the bid, then had returned when the government appeared to have granted noncombatant duty to those in his situation. Instead, he drew the twenty-five years at Leavenworth. (With the end of the war four months later, Wilson ordered him and other conscientious objectors released.) Hugo Gellert, another cartoonist for the monthly, saw a brother jailed for conscientious objection and then shot to death in his military prison in never-explained circumstances. German-American cartoonists were frequent targets of police action on the theory that their avowed pacificism was merely a front for espionage; among those arrested for purported spying were Karl Frederick Widemann and Hans von Stengel, contributors to German-language papers. When the postwar Red Scare added further paranoia to the atmosphere, journals such as the New York *Call* and Milwaukee *Leader* found themselves losing appeals against Burleson's moves as late as 1923.

The end of the war didn't mean the end of timidity for cartoonists employed by the big circulation dailies. On the contrary, given the rush of internal crises afflicting the country over the next twenty years, what followed was one of the dreariest periods for editorial art in U.S. history. Even before the last shot had been fired in Europe, the siege mentality had been tightened still further by the outbreak of the Spanish Lady pandemic and emergency quarantine measures that brought entire cities to a standstill. After that came the first Red Scare, Prohibition and the tommy-gun rule of bootleggers working with the protection of various political machines, the scandals of the Warren Harding administration, the revival of Ku Klux Klan terrorism, the Sacco-Vanzetti case, and the collapse of the stock market. The "normalcy" proclaimed by Harding in 1920 and the "era of tranquility" discerned by his successor Calvin Coolidge a few years later seemed to persuade nobody more than those whose profession was supposed to be watching for the abnormal and making sure nobody got *too* tranquil.

There were exceptions. The Des Moines–based Darling, who had come to his pro-intervention position without official nudging, found next to nobody following him for his equally ardent belief that Congress had to ratify U.S. membership in the League of Nations. Kirby of the New York *World* zeroed in on the hypocrisies of Prohibition with his grubby variation on Uncle Sam designated as Mr. Dry; a representative drawing was "Now, Then, All Together, My Country 'Tis of Thee" from January 17, 1920, in which Mr. Dry, obviously inspired by an 1869 Keppler character known only as Temperance Advocate, stands in front of a giant bottle of water conducting an unseen choir. But it was also Darling and Kirby who, on the heels of the Palmer Raids, contributed some of the more scabrous cartoons justifying the outlawing of the Socialist Party and the deportation of accused radicals; their work carried such titles as "The Bolsheviki Theory of Democracy Is Very Simple" and "Git!"

If there was near unanimity among cartoonists in opposing the Eighteenth Amendment's ban on liquor, there was an equal amount of skittishness among them about the Nineteenth Amendment granting women the right to vote. Even pro-suffrage sentiment was weighed down by thick slabs of condescension. A small handful of women—most prominently Laura Foster, Lou Rogers, Edwina Dumm, and Blanche Ames—managed to break into the male-only profession, but almost always and only for their drawings on the vote question. A 1912 cartoon by Foster in *Life*, for example, depicts a group of militant women shoving members of the National Association Opposed to Woman Suffrage off the top of the globe; another that same year by Rogers in *Judge* depicts Liberty untangling herself from a rope labeled "Politics Is No Place for Women." When the Nineteenth Amendment was finally passed in 1920, the bittersweet consequence was that editors had all the excuse they needed

HUGGING A DELUSION

not to hire more women cartoonists since *their* issue had been resolved. It wasn't until the 1970s, when Etta Hulme was hired by the Fort Worth *Star-Telegram*, that a woman secured a significant staff job as a political cartoonist for a daily paper.

One of the few white cartoonists from a major daily who seemed put out by KKK beatings and lynchings of blacks was Edmund Duffy of the Baltimore *Sun*. It helped that his editor was H. L. Mencken, who was quoted on one occasion as saying "give me a good cartoonist, and I can throw out half the editorial staff." In one of his more noted pieces, "Put It on Again" (January 23, 1928), Duffy pictures a Klansman taking off his hood to reveal the quintessential dimwit and Uncle Sam covering his eyes in fright. What really got under all the hoods and robes, however, was a December 6, 1931, piece entitled "Maryland, My Maryland!"—a mockery of the state song following the lynching of a black man on the Eastern Shore. Maryland dignitaries high and low attacked Duffy, Mencken, and the *Sun* for the suggestion that the state was a racist cesspool; others just attacked—ambushing the paper's delivery vans and beating up drivers. Another exceptional piece was Reginald Marsh's "This is Her First Lynching" from the September 8, 1934, issue of *The New Yorker*; it shows a mother boasting to a friend as she holds her daughter above the heads of a lynch mob.

Closer to the spirit of the times were John Mc-Cutcheon and Herbert Johnson. McCutcheon joined the Chicago *Tribune* in 1903 and stayed there for forty-three

Maryland, My Maryland!

years, serving as a war correspondent as well as a cartoonist. Some have credited him with being the pioneer of the "human interest" cartoon, at least insofar as illustrations heavy on the instant nostalgia of country boys and lop-eared dogs is covered by such a term. Near the end of his career, McCutcheon reflected that he had "always enjoyed drawing the type of cartoon which might be considered a sort of pictorial breakfast food. It had the cardinal asset of making the beginning of a day sunnier."[52] Johnson was the chief cartoonist for the *Saturday Evening Post*, by the 1920s the most popular magazine in America with its estimated one million circulation and five million readers every week. His whimsical treatment of taxation and tariff issues, self-absorbed politicians, and whatever else Washington unleashed were like amiable grousings from a nineteenth-century porch. He would have had no problem with a written claim that "to read the *Post* was to become American, to participate in the American experience."[53]

But then nineteenth-century porches started going under the gavel of twentieth-century bankruptcy auctioneers.

9. New Deals

The cartoonist working between World War I and World War II was anything but the last word in political satire. One big reason was that he was no longer working in the mass medium with the strongest audience pull. With the establishment of national radio networks and the advent of motion picture "talkies," polemical humor had more popular wells than the written word and the illustrated figure. When somebody spoke publicly about "the greatest debunking influence that has come into American public life since the Declaration of Independence,"[54] he was referring to radio, not editorial cartoons. Even on the level of printed caricature, the thriving of such upscale magazines as *The New Yorker* and *Vanity Fair* abetted a celebrity culture in which the exaggerated features of the Gloria Swansons, Charles Lindberghs, and Babe Ruths had far more resonance than those of a Herbert Hoover or Al Smith. Cartoonists were the last ones to disagree with Ruth's widely repeated crack that he deserved more money than Hoover because he had had "a better year."

The heightened expectation of entertainment, if not bedazzlement, hardly promoted deep thinking or profound passions in the representation of gnarled political issues. More than ever, the flash of an image took precedence over its pointedness. Seeking out humorous subjects became more important than seeing complex questions humorously; glibness was all. Most newspaper publishers, already under threat from syndicates moving into local markets and from the consolidation of mastheads, had little patience with against-the-grain views that might compromise their circulation or chill their advertisers. They had created special economic and political affairs sections for adepts, hadn't they? For anybody else who wandered near the editorial page, the Catholic Democratic presidential candidate Smith was a papal spy or wasn't a papal spy, the Wall Street crash meant brokers flying out windows deservedly because they were crooks or tragically because they were victims, and the Great Depression was the defeated cowering on bread lines or selling apples on a street corner. There

weren't all that many illiterates anymore and the immigrant hordes had thinned out, but dumbing down didn't have to be just about literacy, either. It was in this climate that Vaughn Shoemaker of the Chicago *Daily News* could gain renown for his innately overwhelmed John Q. Public character and that a scarred militant like Art Young could question the aims of some of his colleagues. "To have a life as a caricaturist of the kind whose pictures 'never hurt' is my idea of futility," as Young put it.[55]

The arrival of Franklin Delano Roosevelt in the White House was both curse and blessing. It was a curse to the country's major newspaper publishers, who loathed his New Deal policies; it was a blessing for the cartoonists who had the task of conveying that loathing in their work. Like his distant cousin Teddy, FDR possessed outsized physical characteristics that made all the presidents between them a drab interruption to inspiration. His granite-square forehead, aggressive horse teeth, and cigarette holder were delectable illustration fodder. (On the other hand, his wheelchair was seldom portrayed.) Also like Teddy, he was identified with bannered programs (the New Deal) and phrases ("the only thing we have to fear is fear itself") that furnished captions without effort. One cartoon summing up all these tendencies was "The Trojan Horse at Our Gate," a September 17, 1935, drawing by Carey Orr that appeared in the Chicago *Tribune*. The cartoon shows a wooden Democratic donkey with the words "New Deal Tyranny" on its side standing before the wall of a sealed fortress marked "Constitution of the United States." Another piece by Darling for the New York *Herald Tribune* on October 31, 1936, entitled "Halloween 1936," imagines FDR and his aides Harry Hopkins and James Farley as pranksters absconding with a shed marked "Private Rights."

There were dissenters to the anti-Roosevelt onslaught. One was McCutcheon, who refused to illustrate the daily editorial bile in Robert McCormick's Chicago *Tribune*. The fiercely right-wing McCormick's cousin James Patterson got equal grief from Clarence Batchelor at the New York *Daily News*; one Batchelor work from October 11, 1936, "Yes, You Remembered Me," has Roosevelt shaking hands with a grateful laborer identified as "The Forgotten Man." In St. Louis, Daniel Fitzpatrick, Minor's successor at the *Post-Dispatch*, showed complete indifference to the paper's endorsement of such Roosevelt opponents as Alf Landon in 1936. Some of the strongest defenses of the president were by indirection, especially in *The New Yorker*, which almost weekly depicted supercilious high-society types musing how their lives would be much less inconvenienced by a different man in the White House. Then there was Jacob Burck, who contributed his support not only from the left-leaning Chicago *Times* but also from the Communist Party organ, *The Daily Worker*. As odd a minority alliance as this constituted, it proved to be far more in step with the electorate than the big chains and even liberal dailies (most of which condemned Roosevelt's antilabor measures) that were determined to represent the New Deal as a misdeal. It also pushed the cartoonist-as-influence question back yet another degree: If not even the cartoonists working for the most powerful press barons with the widest circulations in the country could prevent voters from putting Roosevelt into office four times, who was paying attention to the editorial page at all? Clearly, not people who were getting an increasing amount of their news from radio (including from FDR directly) and their sense of personality-is-all from the local movie theater.

For the most part, Roosevelt was also able to count on the support of a relatively new cartoon sector—in the black press. The thriving of, among others, the Pittsburgh *Courier*, the Chicago *Defender*, and the Kansas City *Call* gave African Americans a voice they were denied in the white media. This didn't mean a blank check for Roosevelt; especially after his refusal to speak out on behalf of antilynching legislation following the excruciating torching deaths of two blacks in Mississippi in 1937, he was pilloried as much in the *Courier* and the *Defender* as he was in the McCormick and Hearst papers, in this instance for giving priority to keeping Mississippi and the other southern states behind his New Deal programs. But, overall, illustrators of the rank of Oliver Harrington and William Chase of the *Amsterdam News* in New York welcomed his presidency, if only because the alternatives would have been worse. Another graphic pundit was the vibrant painter Romare Bearden, who supplied not only African-American papers but also such magazines as *Collier's* with his early impressions of African-American life in Harlem. In the area of cartooning, though, the dominant figure would prove to be Harrington. His style of holding a sharp knife with a velvet glove was typified by an April 2, 1960, drawing in the Pittsburgh *Courier* in which a whites-only sign on a luncheonette window serves as the background for one black boy to say to another, "My Daddy said they didn't seem to mind servin' him on the Anzio beach head." In 1936, Harrington also created the running character of "Bootsie," a Harlem Everyman who would later trigger some of the same debates about ethnic stereotyping as the enormously popular "Amos 'n Andy" on the radio.

Retrospectivists would also have plenty of meat on their plates from cartoon responses to the rise of Adolf Hitler in Germany and Benito Mussolini in Italy. Initially, the predominant mood in the country was isolationist, with FDR darting behind rhetoric for his agreement with the Republican opposition that "we are not isolationists except insofar as we seek to isolate ourselves from war."[56] For cartoonists, the rule of thumb even years after the Nazis and Fascists had carried out bloody purges and mass confinements within their countries was to treat the dictators as buffoons rather than menaces. This often amounted to discretion over valor since, behind the guise of isolationism, significant sectors of the business community, including those in the media, were not only not too bothered by what was going on in Germany and Italy throughout the 1930s but, in some cases, were profiting from it. The pie-in-the-face approach to Hitler and Mussolini raised the issue—later if not immediately—of the difference between lampoonery and cynical evasiveness disguised as humor.

With the exception of left-wing publications already mobilized by the Spanish Civil War, isolationism turned to nationalism without much of a detour once the United States entered World War II. World War I attitudes and restrictions were reinstituted, this time with the addition of the Japanese as buck-toothed monkeys or any stereotype suggested by the phrase "Yellow Peril." One of the few cartoonists from the mainstream press ahead of the curve was Fitzpatrick, who frequently used the Nazi swastika as a symbol for an engine of death; one

example was his August 24, 1939, drawing "Next," which showed the swastika about to roll over Poland. The cartoon appeared a week before the German invasion that ignited the war. Another who had little doubt about what was coming was Theodor Geisel in his pre–Dr. Seuss career as a cartoonist for the liberal New York daily *PM*. Geisel not only made it clear that Hitler and Mussolini should have been treated far more seriously than as clowns but also extended his warnings to the fascistic America First movement and such group spokesmen as Charles Lindbergh.

Fitzpatrick and Burck of the Chicago *Sun-Times* were also in a decided minority worrying about the FBI's increasing wiretapping of private homes while Roosevelt was making speeches about the "four freedoms" that were assured every American. There was yet less concern about the relocation and internment of tens of thousands of Japanese, Germans, and Italians defined by the FBI as security risks. Even Geisel, who was otherwise militant in his denunciations of racism and anti-Semitism, lent his name to a particularly tasteless *PM* cartoon entitled "Waiting for the Signal from Home" on February 13, 1942. Published mere hours before FDR gave the order to intern Japanese nationals, it showed West Coast Asians (described as "the honorable fifth column") preparing for dynamite attacks while one of their number kept a telescope pointed across the Pacific Ocean for a message to begin sabotage operations.

Neither the European nor the Pacific theater produced startling cartoon work. If one illustrator greeted the German defeat at Stalingrad with Napoleon whispering in the ear of Hitler that he too had failed to conquer Russia, scores did. Bare-skull Death appeared on World

War II battlefields as unimaginatively as it had during World War I. The most original artist to emerge from the war was Bill Mauldin, an infantry sergeant who used his disenchanted characters of Willie and Joe to convey the dogface's daily miseries. Mauldin initiated the series before America's entry into the war, for the *45th Division News* in 1940. In 1943, the series started appearing in *Stars and Stripes* while the illustrator was winning a purple heart in the Italian campaign. When *Stars and Stripes* made a deal with United Features to syndicate what it called "Up Front" back home, the resultant popularity of the strip infuriated General George Patton, who accused Mauldin of undermining military discipline. General Dwight D. Eisenhower took the opposite view, that only attempts to suppress Willie and Joe would have a demoralizing effect, so he arranged to have Mauldin see Patton to smooth over their differences. As the meeting was recounted later by the cartoonist, the general raged at him for making GIs look like "goddam bums" and sneered that "the krauts ought to pin a medal on you for helping them mess up discipline for us."[57] Mauldin weathered the storm and, in 1945, became the youngest recipient of a Pulitzer Prize.

He soon discovered worse enemies than Patton.

10. Cold Wars

Art Young wasn't alone in noticing the tepid quality of political cartoons over the first half of the twentieth century. In the 1940s, historian Allan Nevins delivered himself of the view that "American cartooning since 1890 has shown . . . too many thoughts and too little thought."[58]

For art critic Werner Hofmann, "caricature has paid for its elevation in rank by losing its aggressiveness" and "political caricature's power to wound has diminished, and where caricature is still alive we can see an element of geniality."[59] Already before World War II, William Murrell had been making the case that, for all the respect paid to Nast, he had never had any genuine successors. In his article "Nast, Gladiator of the Political Pencil," Murrell observed, "Nast is often spoken of as the first great American cartoonist. In a very real sense he was the last. For while it is true that many of his symbols and devices have become part of the cartoonist's stock in trade . . . his attitude was a complete flowering of the older tradition—a tradition of ruthless, two-fisted attack."[60]

In 1954, Henry Ladd Smith set off from a similar premise to arrive at a bizarre conclusion. In the May 29th edition of *The Saturday Review*, in a piece that would eventually lead to the formation of the Association of American Editorial Cartoonists, Smith asked whether "the decline of the political cartoon [is] any loss to journalism and the public," immediately answering "not in the opinion of this writer." Why? Because the world had become too difficult for editorial cartoons.

"The cartoonist must tell his story in black and white, literally and figuratively," the journalism professor at the University of Wisconsin declared. "He cannot qualify without weakening impact, and impact is everything to a cartoonist. Yet we know that the complex issues of today can seldom be presented in terms of black and white. Too much misunderstanding has been produced by spokesmen who refuse to qualify charges. If our press is concerned with producing light instead of heat, then the political cartoon doesn't deserve better. . . ."[61]

Aside from showing little regard for the issues that had confronted the country at other junctures in its 170 years, Smith's view encapsulated the 1950s, when any unadulterated opinion apart from anticommunism was considered controversial, if not suspect. It also implicitly romanticized the cartoonists of the past, many of whom might have envied Nast for his keep-away adamance at *Harper's Weekly* but who had never been shy about admitting they could be hired by anybody for any opinion at all. For every Fitzpatrick who refused to follow the *Post-Dispatch* line on Roosevelt or Herblock who took a vacation when the Washington *Post* endorsed Eisenhower against Adlai Stevenson in the 1952 presidential race, there was a Bernhard Gillam attacking Blaine in *Punch* and surreptitiously feeding the pro-Blaine *Judge* ideas for attacking Cleveland. For every Paul Conrad who took a leave of absence when his Los Angeles *Times* got behind Barry Goldwater in 1964, there was a Walt McDougall saying that a cartoonist should have "that curious elasticity of mind that permits him to make cartoons for either party without doing violence to his own opinion."[62] Thanks to his prominence in the Blaine and Pennypacker affairs, even McDougall's malleability wouldn't have sufficed for Currier & Ives. In order to keep catering to one and all, the nineteenth-century lithographers adopted the pseudonym Peter Smith for any partisan cartoon it feared might jeopardize overall sales. Other lithographers fearing commercial retribution simply omitted their signatures.

None of this should have surprised. Leaving aside the pufferies to idealism sent up by a B. O. Flower in *Arena*, cartoonists had always worked within a delineated commercial as well as political system. Originality, out-

landishness, and impact had always been at the service of a periodical seeking more circulation and advertising, a political party seeking to score points against an opponent, or some other interest seeking to ensure one or both objectives. This didn't automatically make individual cartoonists in the mainstream press less passionate about given causes, but it did make the passion a subordinate consideration to those paying the bills—a situation accepted by a pen-for-hire like McDougall.

The hard realities of the cartooning life weren't confined to places of employment. As Charles Press has discovered, some people have been more at ease acknowledging the excellence of political cartoons when they have been able to skip the political part. In a study of the Pulitzer Prizes awarded from 1922 to 1967 (before career achievement became an explicit standard), Press found few sharp polemical drawings surviving nominating committees. What were arguably the two most cutting cartoons to win recognition shared a familiar trepidation of American involvement in foreign affairs. The first, from April 25, 1936, was "Come on in. I'll treat you right. I used to know your daddy," by Batchelor of the New York *Daily News*— a depiction of a hooker labeled "War" enticing a young man identified as "Any European Youth." Equally prophetic was Fitzpatrick's "How Would Another Mistake Help?" in 1954, in which the *Post-Dispatch* illustrator pictures Uncle Sam holding a bayoneted rifle and wondering whether he should follow the French into the mire of Indochina. But even these, Press says, didn't stray *that* far from the acceptable formula:

The appropriate style is to load the cartoon with a symbolism that smacks of unctuousness: a dignified Uncle Sam, or War drawn as

Mars, or Death, or abstract symbols like the burning treaty or the Cross. If these symbols are religious or can be given a Moses smell, so much the better. A recurrent holiness theme hangs over the whole collection [of Pulitzer winners] like cheap incense from the dime store. If high-minded sermons are what is wanted, then cartoonists can supply them, and what would please better than some ecumenical allusion to life's great religious truths?[63]

All of this had made for a lot of pulling at cross-purposes since cartoons had become a big business. But particularly in the years after World War II, many of the profession's internal antagonisms—between the cartoonist's images and the image of the cartoonist, between the priorities of daily newspapers to sell copies

"Come on in, I'll treat you right. I used to know your daddy."

and to lure readers through a distinguishable voice, between the political acuity of the cartoonist and his entertainment function—exploded into the open. Aggravating the situation was the average age of employed cartoonists, many of whom had reached their seventies and even eighties and who had felt a lot more fervid about taking on the Kaiser than they were about going after Joe McCarthy. If the artists faced a special challenge in the late 1940s and 1950s, their ability to be argumentatively nuanced, as cited by Smith, didn't make the Top Ten. The arrival of television not only gave readers something else to do with their eyes than glance at a newspaper illustration but also set off an earthquake of masthead collapses from one end of the country to the other. Cartooning jobs went from scarce to scarcer to scarcest. The cartoonists who held onto theirs became even more cautious about signing off on political visions unpopular in the executive boardroom. If photography had undermined the primacy of physical likeness for cartooning, the face ever present on the small box in the living room raised doubts on second, third, and fourth viewings about whether that caricature in the morning paper had really been that accurate or funny, after all.

Then there were the syndicates, grown into as much of a force as the wire services by midcentury. While providing cartoonists with national visibility, they simultaneously imposed constraints on what should be visible. The local concerns of Portland, Maine were not those of Dallas, Texas. A Cleveland cartoonist's slant on some national policy issue might be boilerplate around Lake Erie but not be so well received in New Orleans. Or, as Universal Press Syndicate editorial director Lee Salem once stated it, "What do readers in San Francisco care about the Omaha sewer system?"[64] The result was still more pressure for blandly treated generic topics so subscribers from Maine to New Mexico could run what they had signed up for. Cartoonists seeking the extra income from the exposure syndication made possible had little choice since standard contracts called for a minimum of four pieces a week dealing with national or international topics.

This did not make them immune to criticism. The lures of syndication were the subject of a Washington *Monthly* article in September 1988 entitled "Why Political Cartoonists Sell Out." Among the findings of veteran cartoonist Lee Judge were that not a single one of forty-nine cartoons published by the Washington *Post* the previous May touched on local D.C. issues, even though the municipal administration of Mayor Marion Barry was being investigated for corruption, and that a mere twelve of three hundred cartoons published by major dailies around the country in the same month dealt with local topics. Judge's conclusion? "Like boys in a locker room, cartoonists are constantly comparing their assets: Who's seen in the most newspapers, who's won the most awards, who makes the most money? Unfortunately, few ask who's brought the most change to their community?"[65]

One who learned syndication's pitfalls the hard way was Mauldin. Only a couple of years away from national acclaim for his Willie and Joe series, he discovered that his attention (he termed it "objective malevolence") to such postwar issues as the plight of the returning GI, racism, and the House Un-American Activities Committee (HUAC) did not please his United Feature Syndicate employers. Writing of the cancellations caused by

his work, he said "it was explained . . . by the syndicate, in a tone reserved for backward children and young men with stirrings of a social conscience, that selling cartoons on a nationwide basis was big business and that it was damn poor business I was doing."[66]

Mauldin's solution was to quit cartooning for almost a decade in favor of writing, working as an actor in Hollywood (John Huston's *Red Badge of Courage*), and even running for Congress in New York. For his part, Walt Kelly fought the economic threats from subscribers to his Hall Syndicate through his "Pogo" comic strip. When the Providence *Journal* dropped the strip to protest a McCarthyish character named Senator Simple J. Malarkey, Kelly not only kept the windbag in but had him

"It Looks Darling"

cover his face with a bag at the approach of a Miss Bombah, a Rhode Island red chicken explicitly identified as coming from Providence. The *Journal* eventually got the message and reinstated "Pogo." Others fared less triumphantly. After the war, Oliver Harrington left daily cartooning for a public relations stint with the NAACP, where he spoke out regularly against racial segregation. When he learned he was being investigated by HUAC, he moved to Paris, where he became an intimate of novelist Richard Wright, then to East Berlin. For almost forty years, he contributed cartoons on American racism to U.S. periodicals from behind the Berlin Wall.

Fitzpatrick and Herblock didn't go anywhere. In an early response to the growing anticommunist fever, the St. Louis *Post-Dispatch* published a Fitzpatrick cartoon on February 23, 1947, that depicted Uncle Sam sitting on a park bench with the Statue of Liberty and saying, "Everyone is a little subversive but thee and me, and sometimes I think even thee. . . ." As the chief cartoonist for the Washington *Post*, Herblock had the advantages and disadvantages of working in the eye of the hurricane. On the one hand, he could be sure that the targets of his government-themed cartoons were taking them in with breakfast every morning in the capital. On the other hand, he had to be careful not to fall into the kind of Beltway mentality that made him more of a court jester than a critic, much as had happened to other cartoonists and numerous columnists in Washington. By his own testimony, he skirted the latter danger primarily by staying away from *Post* editorial conferences, official functions, and even late-breaking news reports that might have tempted him merely to be timely. Just as Fitzpatrick suggested some of Nast in his dedication

"ALAS, POOR AGNEW, MITCHELL, STANS, EURLICHMAN, HALDEMAN, DEAN, KALMBACH, LARUE, MARDIAN, STRACHAN, MCCORD, LIDDY, CHAPIN, HUNT, COLSON, KROGH, MAGRUDER, YOUNG—I KNEW THEM..."

to taking himself *very* seriously, Herblock recalled the deliberateness of the nineteenth-century weekly cartoonist while working for a daily. If hardly ideologically similar, his classically liberal insistence that education and reason had to prevail shared the older man's moral indignation that lunatics were on the verge of taking over the asylum. To keep everyone reminded of that danger, he created Mr. Atom, the symbol of the nuclear threat that hung over U.S.-U.S.S.R. relations. And then Herblock also found his own Boss Tweed.

With the exception of Franklin Delano Roosevelt, no one in American history spent more time in the highest offices of executive government than Richard Nixon. And for every day he was there as vice-president and then president, Nixon had to deal with Herblock. The cartoonist's image of the Republican as a ski-nosed schemer with frail shoulders, angry jowls, and a five o'clock shadow became such a part of the visual language of the twentieth century that Nixon himself was quoted as saying before a presidential election campaign that one of his imperatives was to "erase the Herblock image." Typical of that image was "Here He Comes Now" from October 29, 1954, in which a member of a welcoming committee awaiting the arrival of the then-vice president on the street spots him climbing up from a sewer. For three more decades, through winning and losing elections, through maladroit remarks and pathological deceits, up to the resignation forced by the Watergate scandal, what Fischer has described as the "generic symbol for political venality"[67] was a recurrent image on the *Post* editorial page.

Although Herblock was his most relentless suitor, every prominent cartoonist in the country was attracted to Nixon at some point during a public career that dominated American politics over the last half of the twentieth century. Conrad of the Los Angeles *Times* earned the compliment of being included on the president's infamous "enemies list" (and returned the favor by doting on Watergate scandal developments). The combination of official power and the transparent grasping for still more, wed to a physical presence that sparked wonder he had gotten as far as he had, crystallized cartooning's ideal mix of the infuriating and the absurd. To help out still further, he contributed stock phrases ("Let me make this perfectly clear"), public sulkings ("You won't have Nixon to kick around anymore"), and hilariously solemn disavowals ("I am not a crook"), as well as a mockable middle name (Milhous) that evoked Tweed's

Marcy. Even when Jackson, Lincoln, and the two Roosevelts had elicited contempt from editorial cartoon adversaries, they had remained fundamentally distant, all the more maddening because they were somehow impervious to what was being said (and drawn) about them; Nixon, by contrast, was projected as every family's wheedling cousin who couldn't be left alone in the same room with a pocketbook. "Nixon was to cartooning what Marilyn Monroe was to sex," as cartoonist Doug Marlette once put it. "Nixon looked like his policies. His nose told you he was going to bomb Cambodia."[68]

The reliability of the Nixon image was such that cartoonists could twit themselves for missing him once he had left the White House. Even in private life, however, he continued to beckon as the Godfather, Darth Vader, and other Hollywood villains of the moment. Later presidents were used as excuses for bringing him back to drawing boards. During the 1980 election race, Pat Oliphant drew a desperate Jimmy Carter as a Doctor Jekyll who, looking for a magic formula to overcome Ronald Reagan, transformed himself into a Nixonish Mr. Hyde and smirked, "When the going gets nasty, the nasty get going." In December 1987, Mike Peters of the Dayton *Daily News* played off an announcement by presidential candidate George Bush that he wanted to "sleep on" his choice for a running mate; the Peters cartoon shows a sleeping Bush in his bedroom and the craven Nixon on a ladder outside saying "Niiixxon . . . You waaaant Niiixxxon."

The preoccupation with Nixon as everything that was small and mean about the United States, especially in the late 1950s and early 1960s, wasn't matched by attention to such era-defining developments as the civil rights struggle in the South and the nation's deepening involvement in Vietnam. While a Bull Connor or a Lester Maddox might get drawing pencils going in the wake of some segregationist violence, these remained of a piece with the base personality angle of a "Tricky Dick" rather than as a direct commentary on the larger issues at stake. One of the few exceptions in the mainstream press was Mauldin, who returned to cartooning with the St. Louis *Post-Dispatch* (and later the Chicago *Sun-Times*). By the time most cartoonists swung into action, they found even investigators from the Justice Department there ahead of them.

For Pat Oliphant, arriving in the United States from Australia in 1964, American cartooning was "a laughing stock among other countries of the world" for its avoidance of unpopular positions on knotty issues; "all we ever saw was the Peace Dove with the scroll in its mouth."[69] The Denver *Post* artist didn't think much of the Pulitzer Prizes, either. Confirming Press's findings, Oliphant set out purposely to come up with the kind of illustration that would appeal to the Pulitzer judges, eventually settling on a picture of Ho Chi Minh cradling the body of a dead Vietnamese and saying, "They won't get *us* to the conference table, will they?" His cynicism paid off when he did indeed receive the Pulitzer in 1966 for the drawing.

11. New Societies

Analysts of nineteenth-century cartooning styles have been fond of contrasting Cartoonist A's rapier to Cartoonist B's broadsword and Cartoonist C's stiletto. By the end of the twentieth century, *any* satirical thrust from the customary single-panel political cartoon faced fast blunting. If in theory a single image enlivening the sobriety of a surrounding editorial page could still be incisive, there was also the practicality of absorbing it within a daily avalanche of political mockeries from other media and, for much of the 1960s and early 1970s, from the streets and campuses of American cities. One critic from the period was putting it mildly when he said, "a cartoon is no longer an event, a topic of discussion, as it was in the leisurely nineteenth century."[70] The finer the point made by the cartoonist, the more it sounded like a firecracker amid a howitzer barrage. Even after civil rights and antiwar demonstrations had stopped being an everyday occurrence, after all the elaborately designed placards a Keppler would have envied had been put back in the closet, the cultural mold left behind couldn't easily be reshaped for accommodating the traditional reactiveness of cartoon opinion. Richard Nixon on "Laugh In" wasn't the only one asking to "sock it to me."

As insipid as they could be, the one-liners of late-night TV show hosts and prime-time standup comedians in the 1960s and 1970s were no less biting than most political cartoons. Worse, from the cartoonist's point of view, it was a Johnny Carson crack about Lyndon Johnson's Great Society or Ronald Reagan's jelly beans, not a John Fischetti illustration about either that instigated conversation around the office water cooler in the morning. But television's heaviest weight on cartooning wasn't in the area of relative exposure, which had never been a contest to begin with, but rather in its assumption that politics and politicians *were* just one-liners, that the latest congressional folly was worth recording primarily as a monologue gag. Together with the greater propensity of cartoonists for dealing in television and Hollywood imagery, the dourest senator being berated for the most local of chicaneries came off more as fuel for the entertainment world than as an occasion for passionate political indignation. Around the same time, some dailies began shifting their staff cartoonist off the editorial page to flank gossip columns. Who said seriousness wasn't a rumor, too?

The show business encroachment wasn't an overnight development; the line between editorial cartoon satire and the idly amusing had been blurred for years, and not only because of the conceptual failures of political artists. Cartooning in general had been a puzzle of specializations since the beginning of the twentieth century, when the Oppers had moved over to their Happy Hooligans. With the closing of her editorial cartooning post with the Columbus *Monitor* and the refusal of other newspapers to view her as good for more than suffragette commentary, Edwina Dumm launched her strip with Tippie the dog in 1921. At the turn of the twenty-first century, Jeff MacNelly (Richmond *News Leader* and "Shoe"), Doug Marlette (Tallahassee *Democrat* and "Kudzu"), and Mike Peters (Dayton *Daily News* and "Mother Goose and Grimm") were among those with crossover credits. The strips not only brought artists more money through syndication and book deals, but being placed in the "funnies" section also theoretically relieved them of any obligation to coordinate with editorial page directors political views they were occasionally inspired to stick into the mouths of characters. Many of the tensions in the newsrooms of the late twentieth

century were sparked by differing views on how purely "funny" some of the strips were.

Especially in the 1930s, comic strip artists had freely used their creations as political propaganda battering rams, not least against the Roosevelt White House. The most extravagant case was that of Percy Crosby, whose popular nine-year-old character "Skippy" was gradually steered toward seeking to overthrow "communism, pacificism, prohibition, and gangsterism" in the interests of "returning to American standards." Crosby became so obsessed with his objective that he interpreted as a Marxist conspiracy every cautionary note from Hearst's King Features syndicate about getting Skippy back to the normal pursuits of a nine-year-old. Eventually, the cartoonist who would later be praised as a big influence on such strips as "Doonesbury" and "Calvin and Hobbes" withdrew from drawing to concentrate on privately published books and personal newspaper ads that accused Roosevelt of working for Joe Stalin; after years of conducting his own moral rearmament crusade in between bouts of alcoholism, Crosby died in a mental hospital.

More popular much longer was Harold Gray, whose "Little Orphan Annie" debuted for the New York *Daily News* in August 1924, moved to the Chicago *Tribune* a few months later, and had few equals in voicing the McCormick-Patterson family's hostility toward FDR. At the center of the diatribes was Daddy Warbucks, whose millions were drained from him by Roosevelt's evil income tax auditors and whose attempts to rebound as a self-made man were constantly foiled by lowlifes with names like Slugg and Claptrap. Warbucks's thuggish manner and shaved head reminded more than one reader of Mussolini, and the strip was repeatedly accused of being fascistic. One comic strip creator who saw Roosevelt in a positive light, on the other hand, was Ham Fisher, who drafted the president for an early version of "reality" entertainment during World War II. To beat the drum for military recruitment, Roosevelt was talked into "writing a letter" to his French counterpart requesting the release of Fisher's comic character Joe Palooka from the French Foreign Legion so that he might return to the United States and join the army. The French "acquiesced," after which Palooka's military training became the focus of the strip.

As might have been expected, the World War II adventures of Milton Caniff's "Terry and the Pirates," Zack Mosley's "Smilin' Jack," and other funny sheet heroes were thick with Japanese, German, and Italian stereotypes. By doing little more than filling out cheeks, cartoonists turned the Japanese monkeys into Chinese and Korean monkeys during the Korean War and in later story lines touching on Asian communists; humorless Germans with swastikas on their sleeves became humorless Russians with red stars on their hats. Then there was the increasingly bitter Al Capp of "Li'l Abner." Initially lauded by the likes of Charles Chaplin and John Steinbeck, Capp had moved so far to the right by the 1960s that he was claiming "Little Orphan Annie" creator Gray, whom he had once ridiculed, was more penetrating than Walter Lippmann as a political observer and superior to Picasso as an artist. He didn't take his own professional eclipse too lightly either, insinuating that a Henry Luce publication was involved in a left-wing conspiracy against him. "When I aimed at the right, I was on the cover of *Life*, I was on TV shows," he told the Los Angeles *Times*. "I was the darling of the media. When I took

on the left, I became a leper—except for the people."[71] Capp's final "Li'l Abner" narratives were overwhelmed by smarmy attacks on Joan Baez and the Vietnam peace movement.

Not all the comic strips overlapping traditional political cartooning were right-wing tirades by the aging or the paranoid. No cartoonist of any category, including Nast, has prompted more doctoral theses and essays in learned journals than Kelly for "Pogo." Set in an Oke-fenokee Swamp that had nothing in particular to do with the Georgia location of the same name, Kelly's eponymous possum and friends offered phlegmatic liberal views of the world—at first from the short-lived New York *Star* in the late 1940s (some characters had appeared in an earlier strip centered around the alligator Albert), then later through syndication and in a series of books. The artist's "we have met the enemy and he is us" (originally a 1970 Earth Day poster) didn't stop him from identifying a slew of other enemies in McCarthy, Nixon, FBI chief J. Edgar Hoover, and similar right-wing power figures. This in turn made some syndicate subscribers nervous enough either to suppress installments of the strip or to pull them from the comics section in favor of what was rapidly becoming considered solitary confinement—the editorial page. At its peak in the late 1950s, "Pogo" was syndicated by more than five hundred newspapers for an estimated fifty million readers. In the foreword to the collection *The Pogo Papers*, Kelly described his cartoon world as one in which "traces of nobility, gentleness, and courage persist in all people, do what we will to stamp out the trend."[72]

One of the minor keys of "Pogo" was taking swipes at cartoon strips, including Kelly's own. As modest a part as it played in "Pogo" itself, the self-referential touch illuminated an important aspect of political cartoons at the tail end of the twentieth century. Once upon a time, the Nasts and the Kepplers had included themselves in their drawings for in-panel irony, for the impish suggestion that they were as much part of their cartoon world as of the one where magazines like *Harper's Weekly* and *Puck* arrived in the mail. A hundred years later, there was nothing the least impish about the media's suffusive role in the tableaux of editorial cartoons. Its invasiveness was so total that perceptions of those criticized by it were simultaneously perceptions of those criticized as part of it. Form had never been so interchangeable with content. The cartoonist who didn't acknowledge this more complex reality, who thought a videocam was just a newer Brownie and a televised press conference just a town hall meeting with more outsiders, might have still been *political* in an academic sense, but not very meaningfully beyond that. Sardonic self-references to this state of affairs reflected the media's presumptive position in political events (and in the bargain made completely moot the always tenuous distinctions between political and social satire).

Among the first cartoonists to focus on the media as a primary source of parody were those working for *Ballyhoo* in the early 1930s. One of the humor periodical's standbys was lampooning magazine ads, such as one pitch to women to take a course on how to "Earn Money at Home"; an accompanying photo shows a housewife cleaning out her husband's pants pockets while he sleeps. Another piece mocked newspaper editorials—headlining a page "How Long Shall We Stand For It?" and then inserting such subheads as "Whither?", "What

Next?", and "The People?" to break up the moronic repetition of the single word *blah.* In the 1950s, *MAD Magazine* made pop culture, especially comic strips, movies, and advertising, the target of monthly parodies. When it caricatured politicians, as it did regularly, it was often within the framework of sending up a famous film or popular television show. The periodical's main appeal was to a young audience not normally associated with poring over a daily's editorial page. It was this generation, that later also embraced Garry Trudeau's "Doonesbury."

The first cartoon strip to win a Pulitzer Prize (in 1975), "Doonesbury" has raised more hackles than even "Pogo." When it hasn't been dropped by aggrieved subscribers or exiled to the editorial page, it has brought snippy rebuttals from public figures for perceived mistreatment. Although his drawing board has found room for just about every kind of son and daughter ever to sit down at a family dinner table, Trudeau has saved his sharpest arrows for media types and politicians. He has also borrowed at least one prominent device—symbol as character—from the nineteenth-century cartoonists who, for instance, depicted the colorless President Benjamin Harrison as being lost somewhere under his grandfather William Henry Harrison's high hat. The Trudeau gallery has included House Speaker Newt

Gingrich as a bomb with a lighted fuse, Vice-President Dan Quayle as a feather, the first President George Bush as an empty space, and the second one as an asterisk with a helmet. Moreover, in contrast to the single-shot kind of Harrison illustration, "Doonesbury" has deployed these icons in lengthy narratives.

Trudeau hasn't hesitated to go to words when images have struck him as inadequate to a particularly grim task. On one occasion, he devoted his panels to printing the text of some incriminating testimony against Supreme Court nominee Clarence Thomas that was sneaked into the public record without a witness's personal appearance at a confirmation hearing. Another time, he simply listed the names of all the Americans killed in Iraq while the G. W. Bush White House was doing its best to distract attention from the fatalities. When the first President Bush admitted he had declared a Texas hotel room rather than his Maine or Washington homes as his primary residence in order to avoid state taxes, the cartoonist invited his readers to write to Austin to lodge a similar claim; a reported thirty thousand people took up the invitation. For all that, however, Trudeau has denied being a political cartoonist. "My first aim is to entertain," he has asserted. "Satire is my method, but it's not an end in itself."[73]

Such a protestation is either the kind of grand disingenuousness with which Trudeau has animated some of his characters or a tacit recognition of a peculiar problem created by the intersection of political cartooning and the daily comic strip. Asked once what he thought of the Alan Alda TV series version of his film *M*A*S*H*, director Robert Altman complained that what he had approached as flamboyant human defenses against the horrors of an undeclared war had become on the small screen a weekly acceptance of the UN "police action." According to Altman, the ironically critical attitudes of the TV cast characters were neutralized by the comfort level inherent in the show's regular weekly appointment with triage in the tents, ultimately reducing it in political terms to little more than "Dr. Kildare Goes to the 38th Parallel." The daily strip vis-à-vis the classic editorial cartoon invites a similar thought. When a real politician becomes a stock character in a fictional scenario, no matter how critically he is treated, he enters a protective zone that has little in common with the goals of a potent editorial cartoon; if only to snicker some more, the reader looks forward to the character's return the following day. The objective of the traditional cartoonist, on the other hand, is to draw as forcefully as possible so that the offending politician doesn't return the following day or any other day.

Falling midway between the one-shot editorial panel and the comic strip has been Jules Feiffer. After some years of comic book work, Feiffer brought his (originally-titled) *Sick Sick Sick* to the *Village Voice* in 1956, remaining with the New York weekly for forty-one years before being abruptly told his contract wasn't being

renewed. Feiffer's signature—emulated by scores of others—has been an unbordered sequential set of interior monologues or dialogues barely removed from interior monologues; the lack of defined backgrounds accents the sense of an anchorless world as the contemporary urban characters give voice to their angsts and bafflements. If there is a Freudian flavor to Feiffer's work, it is a Freudianism that has proven as inadequate as any other worldview to dealing with the political and social stresses from, in the cartoonist's words, "people publicly condemning what they privately profit from."[74] If there is a trace of a Mr. Common Man in it, it has the additional color (and pathos) of an Everyman who just might be driven to violence, or at the very least hysteria, by his standing.

Although Feiffer has used a few running characters over the years (the nebbishy Bernard Hergendeiler, the perennially depressed Dancer), most have been transposable suitors of neurosis used for addressing specific issues of the day. This has allowed for dramatizing personal relations in a way a single-panel commentary could not while steering clear of the identifications attached to the narrative arcs of a "Doonesbury." Asked once to characterize his perspective, Feiffer, who has also written award-winning plays and films and won a Pulitzer Prize for his cartooning, said that it probably came down to the fact that "day-to-day living, whether it's in a work situation, in an office, or in a love situation, is as political as running the Pentagon or the State Department."[75]

Feiffer's long connection to the *Village Voice* marked him as the first major cartoonist to attract attention from alternative weeklies. Since then, it has been a rare

resume that doesn't include contributions to, if not staff tenure with, such papers as the Boston *Phoenix*, Seattle *Weekly*, and San Francisco *Bay Guardian*.

A combination throwback and bomb-thrower has been Ted Rall, whose work has been distributed by the Universal Press Syndicate since 1996. Reminiscent of the earliest cartoonists, Rall gained a foothold in New York by posting his drawings on street walls and poles, gaining twelve clients in the process. Once established (also as a radio reporter and writer), he began having to avoid people who wanted to pin him to a wall or ride him out of town on a pole. In 2002, he was harassed by New York City firemen and targeted by right-wing radio ranters for a strip that accused the widows of the victims of the Twin Towers attacks of thinking only about their settlement money. In 2004, the Washington *Post* dropped his cartoons for an effort in which the reelection of George W. Bush was likened to a mentally handicapped student taking over a classroom.

Rall acknowledged he might have gone too far with the student. "The analogy obviously fell flat, or overshadowed the main point of the cartoon," he said. "More importantly, I forgot the editorial cartoonist's obligation to comfort the afflicted while afflicting the comfortable. I got the latter in that cartoon at the expense of the former."[76]

12. Images

For some time now, the political cartoonist has had the aura of the newspaper industry's noble savage. This image has taken shape with the emergence of particularly ravenous competitors (television and the Internet) to newspapers for public attention; the dramatic reduction of cartooning jobs and the increased incidence of cartoonists getting into showdown duels with employers over their work; and the organization of booster trade groups such as the Association of American Editorial Cartoonists (AAEC) for singing the praises of members. Against the background of not merely masthead consolidation but also the global conglomeratization of the mass media, the building theme has been the worsening plight of the righteous and worthy cartoonist within a genre past its prime.

One consequence of these developments has been rhetoric that might have made even Thomas Nast blush if he had resorted to it to justify his attacks on Boss Tweed. It has become de rigueur, for instance, for speakers at the annual AAEC convention to equate the survival of political cartooning with the survival of the press itself. If H. L. Mencken could blithely toss out

the line in the 1920s that one Edmund Duffy was worth half an editorial staff, there was nothing but solemnity behind the claim of long-time Chicago *Tribune* editor James Squires to the *Wall Street Journal* in 1984 that a talented cartoonist "represent[s] the most incisive and effective form of commentary known to man."[77] For Scott Long, the chief cartoonist of the Minneapolis *Tribune*, cartoons were an integral part of "outspoken, courageous, and independent editorial pages [that are] essential to the survival of democracy."[78] Still more basically, historians Stephen Hess and Sandy Northrop see the political cartoon as "the embodiment of the American form of government."[79]

This is a lot of weight to bear, and sometimes sounds like the cry of a blacksmith carrying around a horse to

show everybody how automobiles have nothing on his shoeing work. Even the most explosive recent event involving cartoons—the 2006 riots organized around the world months after several Danish drawings had ridiculed the figure of Mohamed—did not make a new case for the political impact of the genre. On the contrary, it demonstrated only the delayed (if still opportune) political propaganda aims of the Muslim groups behind the protests and, once again, how ethnic and religious stereotypes have been cartooning's most conspicuous field of battle. It was hardly incidental that, behind the banner of free speech, most of the American newspapers publishing the cartoons have had their own caricature problems with Muslims in editorials for years.

But debates about the continued relevance or lack of relevance of the cartoonist tend to obscure the preliminary questions about who, even at the peak of his profession, he has been, what he has truly accomplished, and to what end he has accomplished it. Is the noble savage just an in extremis continuation of the earlier romance about the cartoonist as a St. George ready to take on all dragons? The record has been pretty clear on this latter image. As with any other work category in or out of the mass media, there have been relatively few valiant knights. Except for the Herblocks, Mauldins, and a few others, cartoonists over the years have generally done what they have been told to do or anticipated being told to do, or they have not had the imagination to improve on what it had been a bad idea to do. One reason the Fitzpatricks and Conrads have stood out is that they *have* been exceptions.

It is no surprise that the contemporary cartoonists with the most acerbic visions and sharpest pens to express them—the Marlettes, Ralls, and Steve Bensons—have figured prominently in the newsroom controversies of recent years that have triggered firings, resignations, and eliminations of cartooning jobs. Even excluding the pressures brought to the profession by national syndication priorities, the growth of local lobby groups and ad hoc committees hungry for camera time has insured that even the faintest of perceived offenses is only a cell-phone protest away. Some newspapers have defended their artists all the way to court, but many more have truckled under to bullying that has confirmed the editorial point made by the cartoonist in the first place. And even the fact that lawsuits have fallen off since the beginning of the new century is not necessarily reason for jubilation. As Chris Lamb has observed,

This does not mean that cartoonists are freer to draw their conclusions without being sued—or even that their newspaper will support them. Instead, there may be fewer lawsuits brought against cartoonists because fewer daily newspapers have fewer editorial cartoonists, who are drawing fewer local cartoons. In addition, rather than defending themselves in court, newspapers are settling lawsuits, suppressing cartoons, or simply not publishing local cartoons."[80]

Also because of a select handful of artists, there has been a perception that the cartooning fraternity has always been dominated by those on the left of the political spectrum. When such conservatives as Jeff MacNelly, Tom Curtis, and Mike Ramirez started drawing attention between the 1970s and 1990s, some overviews of the profession treated this development as a startling turn in relations between newspaper art departments and political officialdom. This would have come as news to the generations of cartoonists who did little to disturb the political status quo during the minimally interrupted half-century of Republican rule between Lincoln and William Howard Taft, who fell asleep altogether between Woodrow Wilson and Franklin Delano Roosevelt, who had red flags waved for them in front of FDR, and who kept saluting Eisenhower with the trembling hope that he really *was* better than Nixon and McCarthy. It wasn't until cartoonists of all stripes got caught up as much as everybody else in the Camelot fancies of the John F. Kennedy presidency that there was an appreciable lessening of knee-jerk antagonism in the mainstream press toward a Democratic chief executive just because he was a Democrat. That carried over after Kennedy's assassination to the point that artwork critical of his abbreviated term was excluded from some cartoon book collections. It did not carry over to Lyndon Johnson, who even before he was being toasted for his Vietnam policies was a daily target of the right for his Great Society initiatives.

Of course, cartoonists themselves have never been enthusiastic about relating the tilt of their work to formal political affiliations. Aside from those employed by official party organs or satellite organizations, such as the Minors and Youngs, the most conspicuous exceptions to this have been the Volcks, with their fiercely declared (and brutally demonstrated) allegiance to the South during the Civil War, and the Nasts, who have portrayed temporary defections from specific parties as the necessary consequence of a personal betrayal. In both cases, in being honored and in being broken, preemptive loyalties have been brandished as a moral more than a political high ground. Otherwise, even the most obviously aligned cartoonist will insist he is only drawing what he sees, with no a priori commitments to anybody, a thoroughly independent soul on the job. It thus commanded attention when not one but two cartoonists broke publicly with this tradition around the 1980 presidential elections.

For Don Wright of the Miami *News*, there was far too much truth in the Herblock crack that "a vote for Carter or Reagan is a vote for Carter or Reagan." "I'm flat out for [independent] John Anderson and I'm going to try in my cartoons to get him elected," Wright confessed at the time. "I'm going to do this by not criticizing John Anderson. I will ignore his indiscretions and concentrate on the big boys."[81] MacNelly had the same kind of commitment—but deeper doubts—following Reagan's election in 1980. "He had an agenda, and I was behind him," the Richmond *News Leader* artist admitted. "That was hard for me because I hate to do cheerleading cartoons. . . . I can't go around saying, 'Gee, isn't the president doing a great job?' That's not what a political cartoonist does."[82]

At his best, he doesn't manufacture targets, either. The cartoonist as a constitutional contrarian, attacking issues or officials just for the sake of attacking them because he doesn't have anything else working in his brain, has seldom produced a magical moment; just the opposite, that approach has generated the numerous bleak examples of cartoonists piling on some foe of an employer, servicing some government propaganda line, or just filling out a timecard. A minimal premise of good cartooning has been a cause that, unlike Press's estimate of Frank Bellew, *did* excite the cartoonist. Or, as Herblock has described this function,

. . . a good explanation [of cartooning] is in the story of the school teacher who asked the children in her class to give examples of their kindness to birds and animals. One boy told of how he had taken in a kitten on a cold night and fed it. A girl told of how she had found an injured bird and cared for it. When the teacher asked the next boy if he could give an example of his kindness to nature's creatures, he said, "Yes, ma'am. One time I kicked a boy for kicking a dog."[83]

For the most forceful cartoonists, the boy to be kicked has never been primarily a Democrat or a Republican, but an institution that has tolerated idiocies, abuses, or greeds flaunted as patriotism; never been an individual politician, but a society of misrule that has produced repressive practices and abominable laws; never been a Tweed or a Nixon, but all the human hustlings and meannesses personified by them. In short, the boy to be kicked (and why not have a little fun doing it?) has been power and its exercise. In the United States, the most immediate institution structuring the daily practice of political power has been the two-party system, irrespective of which of the parties has been dominant in a given period. To caricature, satirize, and otherwise question that system rather than either of its separate components implies not a liberal or conservative viewpoint, but a radical one. The fact that the work of the Feiffers, Kellys, and Trudeaus has been far more explicit about excoriating the overall system's costs, decays, and corruptions, while most conservative commentary has lived up to its name by being preoccupied with the internal ideals of a Republican soul and the deficiencies of a Democratic one, has by apology and alibi left tinted as liberal the most comprehensively critical cartooning of recent years.

As a reactive journalistic profession, cartooning has never been expected to be ahead of the curve artistically,

to pioneer an aesthetic vision. The more unfamiliar the graphic approach, the less the public is likely to grasp the polemical point within the few seconds normally spent on a newspaper drawing. Paradoxically, in other words, the more reassuring elements there are in a cartoon, the clearer the message that there is nothing at all reassuring about the situation being denounced. Nevertheless, personal style—whether it be the simple line drawings in bold strokes Nast learned from England's Tenniel or the grease pencil techniques Minor and Robinson passed on to a generation of cartoonists—remains the criterion for distinguishing the artist from the hack. Which is more memorable: any of the thousands of naturalistic renderings of George W. Bush to be found anywhere sketchbooks are sold or Trudeau's asterisk with a helmet? Ed Stein, a long-time cartoonist for Denver's *Rocky Mountain News*, has little doubt, acknowledging with glum candor,

With the exception of a handful of artists who have made a conscious effort to develop a distinctive graphic style, our drawings,

with minor stylistic differences, look pretty much alike. . . .
We've become like a huge family of identical siblings; we can tell
each other apart at a glance, but nobody else can.[84]

But as potent an alliance as polemic lucidity and artistic strength can make, it is still at the mercy of a distribution vehicle for gauging its impact, and even great
circulation is no automatic synonym for great influence.
One venerable point of view is that cartoons have not so
much altered the thinking of those exposed to them as
merely reinforced previously existing values and biases.
Nast's treatment of Tweed, for instance, might have
helped triple the circulation of *Harper's Weekly*, but only
in a decidedly vicarious key: the new subscribers came
primarily from parts of the United States having no electoral say in New York City or New York State. Similarly, a
decade and a half of anti-Nixon cartoons from newspapers coast to coast did not prevent his election to the
White House in 1968 or reelection in 1972.

But if cartoonists have always just been preaching to
the choir, not only in emphatically ideological periodicals along the lines of *The Masses* but in the mainstream
press as well, the question goes back to how indispensable they have truly been. Have they been only an entertainment all along, with congressmen and presidents

taking the role of mothers-in-law for the joke telling?
Have we merely been a variation on all those pols at the
turn of the twentieth century who wanted to crack down
on cartoonists—insisting on the *perception* of their significance in order to congratulate ourselves for always
having had a vigilant press? When all the dust has settled
from the blowups between editorial directors and art
departments over slants on a given issue, have cartoonists still delivered only graphic versions of the self-
important editorials newspapers print every day to no
surprise or fascination? Ultimately, is their function
just to provide layout variety, offering a change of pace
from words, photos, and advertisements?

Then there is this: Has the recent applause for cartoonists grown in inverse proportion to the spontaneous
laughs they have elicited, much the way the Lettermans,
Lenos, and Stewarts on their late-night TV shows pro-
voke clapping rather than giggling for their quips because approval for the predictable has taken precedence
over openness to effective insight? Herblock, for one,
worried about just such a reception where his Mr. Atom
was concerned. "I felt a good deal of satisfaction when
people used to tell me, with flattering exaggeration, that
the Atom character gave them the shivers," he once said.
"But when I began hearing about 'that cute Mr. Atom you
draw,' I gave him longer rest periods."[85]

On occasion, defenses of the cartoonist's irreplace-
ability have sounded like pleas for keeping the game going for its own sake. Thus "Calvin and Hobbes" creator
Bill Watterson was once moved to the observation that
"people do not turn to cartoonists to learn what to think.
Rather they turn to cartoonists to be confronted with an
opinion—one that could just as easily be unpalatable as

such a modest assessment of his function? Since when has a civil exchange of opinion been a cartooning hallmark?

Once upon a time, cartoonists weren't shy about biting the hand that fed their rivals. In peak periods of competition between magazines and newspapers in the nineteenth century, sniping back and forth was all but mandated. Among the subscription weeklies there was little apprehension about affording a rival and his publisher free publicity; the political capital to be made from ridiculing a Nast or Keppler for a perceived gaffe accrued completely to the aggressor. Among the daily newspapers the attacks were usually more organizational than personal—not Davenport the fool, but the New York *Journal* the fool. With the small literary and ideological magazines of the first part of the twentieth century, especially those of a Marxist bent, the cartooning targets weren't so much individual papers as the mainstream press as a whole, viewed as part of the institutional problem.

Ironically, many mainstream cartoonists who would have developed a rash if accused of being socialists came around to a similar comprehensive critique later in the century when they went after the electronic media for representing *in se* everything that was unholy about American society. Whether it was the quiz show scandals of the 1950s, the presidential election debates of the 1960s and 1970s, or the "reality show" Iraqi wars waged in the 1990s and the new millennium, suddenly there was fretting not just about television's specific content but also about its intrinsically manipulative impact on the information it purveyed. The print media making the accusations were normally exempt from the critique,

lending a defensively professional dimension to a grave social observation.

The fact is that political cartooning has repeatedly shown an inability to get out of its own way. At first, this took the form of cartoonists crowing about their own importance within their work; later on, the depressive air that was never too far from the boasting began to assert itself. In the words of cartoonist Mike Peters, "writers grow up to be editors, cartoonists just grow up to be old cartoonists."[87] The profession's respected AAEC forum was founded as a direct result of the 1954 Ladd Smith *Saturday Review* article that counseled cartoonists to pack up their pencils and look for another career. To a near pathological degree, AAEC literature regularly churns out articles with titles such as "Do We Still Matter?"[88] *Maus* creator and comic book innovator Art Spiegelman didn't sound at all novel in 1999 when he observed that "over the past twenty to thirty years the newspaper editorial cartoon has reduced its ambition, basically becoming a gag cartoon with political subject matter."[89] When asked why there weren't more women in the political cartoon business, Signe Wilkinson of the Philadelphia *Daily News* borrowed some glibness from the same state of disenchantment: "Perhaps it's just because women consider that going into a shrinking field in which depressed men get up every day to make fun of people and then see whether their creations have made it into *Newsweek* isn't the most productive way to use their few precious moments on the planet."[90]

Looked at too deeply, some of the genre's newest outlets don't promise revolutionary tomorrows, either. Happily for many cartoonists caught up in newsroom conflicts, they have been able to maintain contact with the public through personal and group websites; but even their high-ranked Google name value doesn't offer the same exposure for potential impact that print does. More to the political point, aside from needing a password to get on-line, how different is website cartooning (not to mention the recent passion for blog cartooning) from the broadsides that were once posted in very local colonial taverns? Does the animated political cartoon bring a new, more involving format for keeping issues in front of the public or simply another franchise for the Walt Disney vision of the world? Is the trend by dailies such as the Los Angeles *Times* toward deinstitutionalizing the editorial page a true incentive for eliciting broader opinion, including the graphic kind, or just another pusillanimous development similar to phone-in radio for appeasing advertisers under the cover of promoting greater popular participation?[91] Have we heard the last of attempts by private corporations to send their own cartoons to editorial pages, the way Mobil Oil did in the 1970s to criticize various government policies? Do the ever more numerous gallery exhibitions paying tribute to cartoonists present and past—or, for that matter, the greater speed at getting their work into book form—honor the artist at the expense of his supposed political role?

The answers to these questions lie not only with the future direction of the mass media that accounted for the blossoming of cartooning to begin with but also with the emergence of artists politically savvy enough to realize they don't have to insert themselves into their panels because they are already there and graphically original enough to move even one odd reader every once in awhile beyond the social attitudes he brought to the newsstand. Otherwise, the history of cartooning is doomed to be nothing more than the history of cartooning.

1

Presidents

The election of a president is supposed to set the political tone for four years; it certainly sets the cartooning tone for that time. From the vanished illustration of George Washington on a jackass to the vanished head of George W. Bush under a helmet, chief executives have served as the editorial cartoonist's shorthand for four years of policy snafus, official gaffes, and government deceits. More than the framers of the Constitution ever intended, the president *is* the government for political illustrators—not as the First Administrator or as the last stop for the passing of the buck but as the directly involved commander-in-chief in all things military and civilian, domestic and international. However fanciful this perception has been in many cases, it has meant extra homework at the drawing board for distilling the prime personality of every administration. "Cartoonists are after that certain quality that comes through despite everything that makeup artists, speech writers, spin doctors, and press secretaries do to hide it," in the words of Doug Marlette. "We want his soul."[92]

By cartooning standards, the greatest presidents have been Jackson, Lincoln, the two Roosevelts, Nixon, and Reagan. Kennedy had been well on his way to joining this select circle for everything from his youthful, ener-getic looks, phrase-making ("Ask not what your country can do for you . . . ," "*Ich bin ein Berliner*"), and political crises (the Bay of Pigs, the Cuban missile crisis) to his Hollywood cronies (Frank Sinatra and the Rat Pack) and the promotion of the Camelot image, when his assassination drew a veil over his presidency. Meriting honorable mention have been Jefferson, for serving when editorial cartoons and their means of distribution were still at a fairly primitive level, and Bill Clinton, for opening inkwells to all the dreary sex jokes that had been co-agulating since Cleveland dodged questions about how many children he had fathered.

The worst presidents have been all those who brought the country to the edge of some precipice, but without idiosyncratic panache. If they weren't sufficiently grace-less physically or were too successful at keeping dubious confidants behind the curtain, they maintained just the right level of stagnant leadership so this deficiency alone didn't become a lampoonable trait. Massive corruption affairs, for example, didn't earn Grant an indelible image, any more than brutal expansionism gained one for McKinley. Somewhere in the middle were those who had extraordinary qualifications in just one category, such as the elephantine William Howard Taft. With

Taft's departure from the scene, poet-caricaturist Oliver Herford lamented, "I'm sorry William Taft is out / Of Politics; without a doubt / Of all the Presidential crew / He was the easiest to do."[93]

Not counting FDR, who died in office, cartoonists have been reluctant to forget their favorite targets when these have moved on from Washington to their memoirs. In great part because of newspaper art departments, John Wilkes Booth ended up abetting Lincoln's rise to the level of a national symbol. In the cases of Teddy Roosevelt and Nixon, the Oval Office was little more than a through station for cartooning attention. Not even an assassination attempt and a cancer episode discouraged cartoonists from going after Reagan for his shoe-polish black hair, Hollywood background, and the perception that he was merely "playing" the chief of state from a script written by his advisors and wife. Trudeau was particularly aggressive in a comic strip story arc around the theme of archeologists looking for Reagan's brain. Other graphic fodder was furnished by the "Evil Empire" speech delivered before the British House of Commons in 1982, the bizarre U.S. invasion of Grenada in 1983, and the Irangate disclosures in 1987.

Nancy Reagan was one of several First Ladies who offered as much of a target as a sitting president. At that, her widely portrayed Wasp Woman personality came off as a compliment compared to the often vicious treatment of the wives of Andrew Johnson, Wilson, and FDR, among others. (American cartoonists were following in the tracks of some British counterparts, who labored at deriding Washington as a woman disguised as a man during the War for Independence and his presidency.)

The main theme of the cartoon attacks on the wives was that they exerted undue influence over the decisions of their husbands—a personalized variation on the snickering that greeted the suffragette and women's liberation movements. In the particular case of Eleanor Roosevelt, her championing of liberal causes also left her vulnerable to McCarthyites in the Cold War climate of the late 1940s and 1950s.

The losers of presidential election races had little reason to expect mercy, and they didn't get much. Their one consolation in most cases was that they ceased being politically vital after failing to gain the White House and so faded away as cartoon targets fairly rapidly. That didn't spare three-time loser William Jennings Bryan, whose energetic rise and pathetic fall in public life over a languid thirty-four years was chronicled meticulously by artists from one end of the country to the other.

Responses from targets varied. Nixon was so harassed by Herblock that he announced he was canceling his subscription to the Washington *Post* in the name of protecting his daughters. By contrast, Theodore Roosevelt boasted of having a collection of the attacks on him, even hanging one in his White House office that predicted he would never make a credible president. Lyndon Johnson was also known to have emissaries contact the Washington *Post* for adding to his Herblock trove. Reagan sought to make light of the cartoon attacks on him, but this was only after, as governor of California, he had gotten into the habit of calling Los Angeles *Times* publisher Otis Chandler to protest the latest Paul Conrad illustration. When Chandler began avoiding the calls, Nancy Reagan took over from her husband until she too always found Chandler on another line.

THE PROVIDENTIAL DETECTION

In its bitter attack on Jefferson, PROVIDENTIAL DETECTION (1800) also marked the first conspicuous appearance in cartoons of the eagle as a national symbol. *The Granger Collection, New York.*

David Claypool Johnson's PRESIDENTIAL CAMPAIGN (1824) was typical of the cartoons that approached presidential elections as sporting events. In this one, the runners were John Quincy Adams, William Crawford, and Andrew Jackson. *The Granger Collection, New York.*

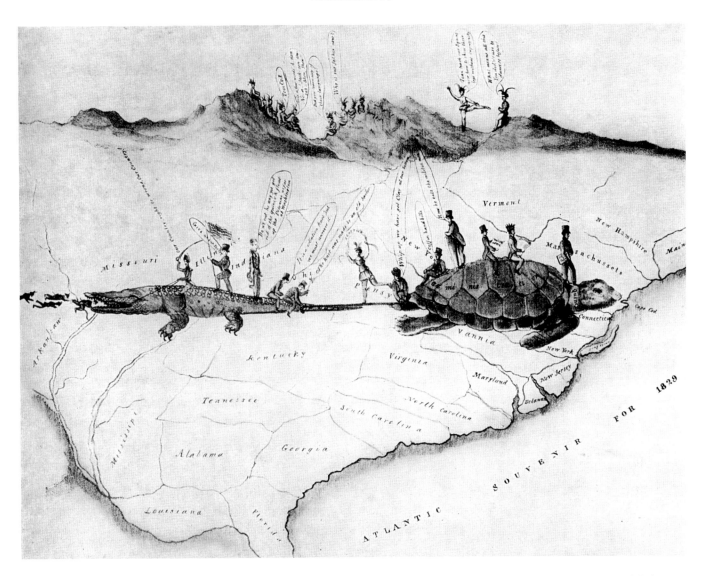

The first American political cartoon produced through lithography carried the garrulous title of A NEW MAP OF THE UNITED STATES, WITH THE ADDITIONAL TERRITORIES ON AN IMPROVED PLAN (1829). Printed by Anthony Imbert, it symbolized the 1828 election race between Andrew Jackson (the alligator) and John Quincy Adams (the turtle). *The Granger Collection, New York.*

BORN TO COMMAND.

OF VETO MEMORY.

HAD I BEEN CONSULTED.

KING ANDREW THE FIRST.

Lithographers had a field day with the scandal brought down on the Jackson administration by the shady past of Peggy Eaton, the wife of the war secretary. When Jackson couldn't persuade his Cabinet members to get their wives to accept Eaton socially, he dismissed the whole cabinet for a new group of advisers. The fact that Eaton never actually appeared at any White House gathering to discuss her situation didn't stymie this anonymous cartoonist (1836). *The Granger Collection, New York.*

◁ BORN TO COMMAND: KING ANDREW THE FIRST (1832) was a typical attack on Jackson turned out by lithographers in the early 1830s. *The Granger Collection, New York.*

UNCLE SAM SICK WITH LA GRIPPE.

UNCLE SAM SICK WITH LA GRIPPE (1837) is the only known instance of Uncle Sam (in the chair) and Brother Jonathan (outside the window) being depicted together. *The Granger Collection, New York.*

THE DOWNFALL OF MOTHER BANK (1833) pictured Andrew Jackson
and his faithful shadow Brother Jonathan watching National
Bank president Nicholas Biddle and his Whig supporters taking
a fatal tumble. *The Granger Collection, New York.*

THE MODERN BALAAM AND HIS ASS (1837) marked the real debut of the donkey as a Democratic symbol. *The Granger Collection, New York.*

John Childs's lithograph features an anti-Jackson version of Major Jack Downing watching from behind the door of NOTICE TO QUIT (1841) as Martin Van Buren hurries away from the White House in favor of William Henry Harrison. *The Granger Collection, New York.*

THE NATIONAL GAME. THREE "OUTS" AND ONE "RUN".

Baseball was a popular sporting motif for Currier & Ives, as in this 1860 Louis Maurer cartoon depicting Lincoln's victory over campaign opponents John Bell, Stephen Douglas, and John Breckinridge. *The Granger Collection, New York.*

Adalbert Volck's contempt for Lincoln had no expiration date. ☞ His PASSAGE THROUGH BALTIMORE in 1863 depicted the president's supposedly cowering trip to Washington two years earlier amid reports of an assassination plot. *The Granger Collection, New York.*

LINCOLN SIGNING THE EMANCIPATION PROCLAMATION.—FROM A SOUTHERN WAR ETCHING

Volck saw little conscience involved in Lincoln's signing of the Emancipation Proclamation. *The Granger Collection, New York.*

Nast's COMPROMISE WITH THE SOUTH (1864) was regarded as a vital contribution to Lincoln's reelection. The artist's wife posed for the woman grieving over the grave. *The Granger Collection, New York.*

"WE ARE ON THE HOME STRETCH."—*New York Tribune*, October 9, 1872.

WE ARE ON THE HOME STRETCH was Nast at his nastiest, using
death themes to attack the recently widowed and frail Horace
Greeley during the 1872 election. *The Granger Collection, New York.*

Keppler's THE MODERN WANDERING JEW (1880) portrayed Grant ☞
as desperately leaning on his war record in seeking an unprecedented third White House term. *The Granger Collection, New York.*

THE MODERN WANDERING JEW.

A fated wanderer, his way he wends,   Where'er he goes, sign of a people's wrath,
Driven here and there by many selfish friends;   The Curse of the Third Term still haunts his path.

Bernhard Gillam's PHRYNE BEFORE THE CHICAGO TRIBUNAL (1884)
was one of two hard blows delivered to the presidential aspirations of Republican James Blaine. *The Granger Collection, New York.*

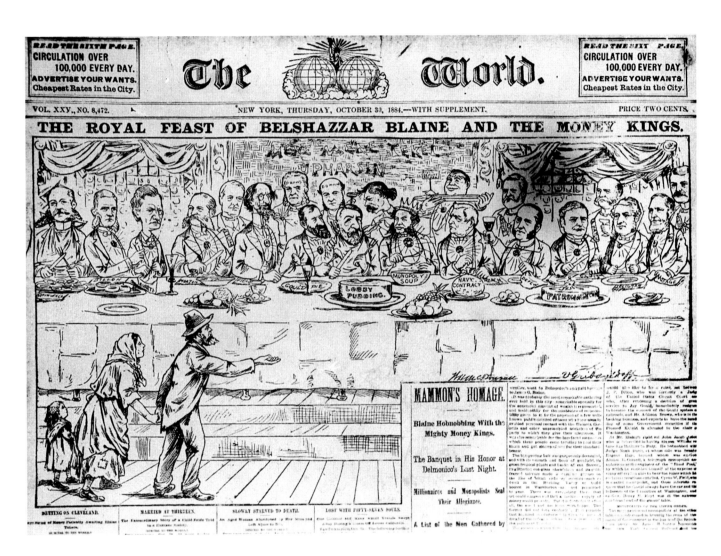

The Walt McDougall cartoon on the front page of the New York *World* that helped doom James Blaine's presidential aspirations (1884). *The Granger Collection, New York.*

Another voice for Cleveland.

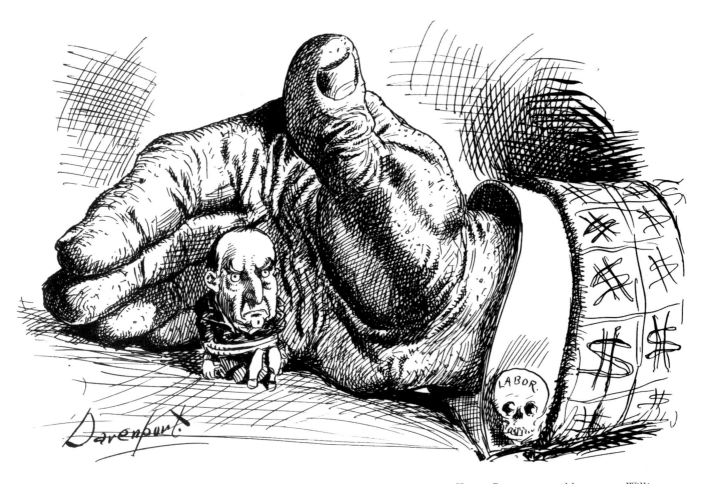

Hearst cartoonist Homer Davenport could never see William McKinley as other than a Mark Hanna plaything (1890s). *The Granger Collection, New York.*

Frank Beard's ANOTHER VOICE FOR CLEVELAND (1884) was part of the Republican campaign to take down the Democratic candidate after he admitted that he might have had a child out of wedlock and, one way or the other, had paid to support the boy until his adoption. *The Granger Collection, New York.*

In the eyes of Joseph Keppler, Benjamin Harrison would always be on the verge of vanishing inside the hat of his grandfather William Henry Harrison (1892). *The Granger Collection, New York.*

Grant Hamilton provided the most noted graphic image of the
"Cross of Gold" speech that William Jennings Bryan rode to the
Democratic presidential nomination in Chicago in 1896. *The
Granger Collection, New York.*

IF (1904) was J. S. Pughe's vision of how William Randolph Hearst, the newspaper world's chief promoter of comic strips, would celebrate at the White House if he ever realized his presidential ambitions. *The Granger Collection, New York.*

Theodore Roosevelt's reputation as a trust buster didn't ☞ persuade everyone: in this 1904 piece, he is depicted ordering Attorney General Philander Chase Knox to go easy on the monopolies because it was an election year (1904). *The Granger Collection, New York.*

Woodman, spare that tree;
Touch not a single bough.
Funds would be scarce if we
Should "run amuck"—just now.

With DRAWING THE LINE IN MISSISSIPPI (1902), Clifford Berryman not only provided a sensitive image for Teddy Roosevelt but also inspired one of the world's most popular toys. *The Granger Collection, New York.*

Louis Glackens pictured a consumer fancying a positive side to William Howard Taft's enormous torso—that its sheer weight might lower the cost of living. *The Granger Collection, New York.*

WOODROW WILSON, THE SCHOOL TEACHER.

Woodrow Wilson's teaching background was frequently invoked
for cartoon commentary, such as during the 1914 U.S. moves
to install friendly governments in Mexico, Venezuela, and
Nicaragua. *The Granger Collection, New York.*

Clifford Berryman portrayed Democrat Al Smith and Republican Herbert Hoover as galloping off to solicit votes in their most vulnerable areas during the 1928 election. *The Granger Collection, New York.*

The Bonus Army newspaper compared Herbert Hoover to a Prussian militarist for his deafness to Bonus Army marchers in 1932. *The Granger Collection, New York.*

Clifford Berryman's NEW DEAL REMEDIES (1935) was noteworthy
for a rare cartooning appearance by an Aunt Sam. *The Granger
Collection, New York.*

Ben Shahn's A GOOD MAN IS HARD TO FIND, a propaganda poster for the Progressive Party in the 1948 elections, satirized a noted photo of the period showing Harry Truman playing the piano for actress Lauren Bacall. Shahn substituted Thomas E. Dewey for Bacall in the pitch for a third electoral option. *The Granger Collection, New York.*

Bill Mauldin's view of the John F. Kennedy assassination became
the most noted cartoon response to the killing. *Copyright 1963.
Chicago Sun-Times, Inc. Reprinted with permission. Reproduction
prohibited.*

"Here He Comes Now"

Nixon emerging from a sewer became a milestone in Herblock's treatment of the Republican leader. From *Herblock: A Cartoonist's Life* (Times Books, 1998).

Paul Conrad's portrayal of Nixon as Hamlet was one of scores of
cartoons the *Los Angeles Times* artist devoted to the Watergate
scandal. *Copyright 1973 Paul Conrad/Los Angeles Times.*

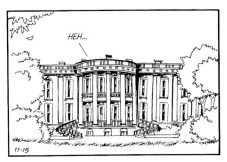

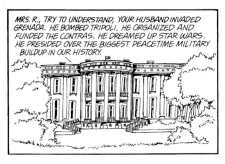

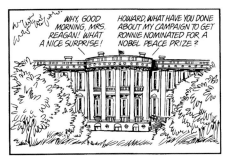

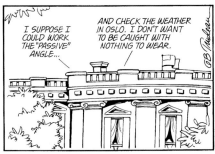

Nancy Reagan's Wasp Woman image was a favorite motif for "Doonesbury." *Doonesbury © 1987 G. B. Trudeau. Reprinted with permission of Universal Press Syndicate. All rights reserved.*

For Doug Marlette, the 1980 election race came down to a choice between Jimmy Carter's Cowardly Lion and Ronald Reagan's Tin Man. *Copyright 1980 Marlette/The Charlotte Observer.*

Trudeau used the popularity of the Indiana Jones movies as a springboard for his Searching for Reagan's Brain series. *Doonesbury © 1987 G. B. Trudeau. Reprinted with permission of Universal Press Syndicate. All rights reserved.*

Paul Conrad's ᴀꜰꜰɪxɪɴɢ ʙʟᴀᴍᴇ ꜰᴏʀ ᴏᴜʀ ᴇᴄᴏɴᴏᴍɪᴄ ᴘʀᴏʙʟᴇᴍꜱ ☞ updated a noted Thomas Nast motif in attacking the Tweed ring to every president from Washington to Reagan. *Copyright 1982 Paul Conrad/Los Angeles Times.*

AFFIXING BLAME FOR OUR ECONOMIC PROBLEMS

Ariail's take on the 1996 election race among Republican Bob Dole, sitting president Bill Clinton, and the independent Ross Perot. *Copyright 1996 Robert Ariail/The State.*

For Joel Pett, Florida's compromised role in the 2000 elections helped make the Bush administration's pronouncements on terrorism mere rhetoric. *Copyright 2001 Joel W. Pett, Lexington Herald-Leader. Reprinted with permission.*

2

Wars and Foreign Relations

Until recently in the mainstream press, wars counted imaginative cartooning among their casualties. Thanks to instituted censorship, political intimidation, or personal conviction, few cartoonists found it necessary to dish up anything but unadulterated propaganda and the crudest of chauvinist sentiments during periods of foreign engagement. A basic ingredient of this outlook was depicting entire peoples (the enemy) as subhuman species, making their destruction easier to rationalize. During the Civil War, Volck and others showed that this same attitude could be applied to internal conflicts.

There were exceptions. With New England commercial interests up in arms over embargoes against British goods, the period immediately up to and through the War of 1812 generated a great deal of skeptical artwork about the early-nineteenth-century hostilities. Not only Volck and his similars in the South but also Democratic-controlled periodicals in the North never tired of attacking Lincoln's prosecution of the War between the States—at least until he began making martial-law moves toward shutting them down. In the twentieth century, even before the fork in the road known as Vietnam, the Korean conflict attracted enough criticism from cartoonists and the press in general that General Charles

Willoughby, the intelligence chief on General Douglas MacArthur's staff, railed to a national magazine that "these ragpickers of modern literature, roughly between belles-lettres and the police blotter, have developed an insufferable but peculiarly American characteristic: they have come to believe they are omniscient."[94]

Between the middle of the nineteenth and twentieth centuries, most opposition to U.S. engagements abroad was driven by isolationism rather than by some principled resistance to enlarging American influence through force of arms. But even in cases of ideological contrariety cartoonists displayed far more creative edge when expressing their apprehensions prior to an actual outbreak of hostilities; once armies went on the march, glib pieties masking resignation descended on art studios. Death scything its way through corpses, the Four Horsemen of the Apocalypse, and butchered women and children strewn across the battlefield were recurrent motifs during World War I and World War II, and not too often to ringing effect. In fact, the resort to a mythological symbol such as Death or the Devil generally proved counterproductive to the cartoonist's presumed intention in the most basic way conceivable, by dehumanizing the casualties. In addition, the abstract component of cartoon commentary rarely equaled the immediate vivid reality of photographs making a similar point. For example, no cartoon ever had the impact—emotional *or* political—of the photographs showing the heaps of mangled skeletons disinterred from Nazi concentration camps.

Since Vietnam, there has been far more cartooning criticism in the mainstream press of American overseas military adventures, much of it spurred by skepticism, when not outright disbelief, at the official reasons for dispatching troops. What had been a murmur in Grenada and Haiti grew to a chorale by Bosnia and, especially, the invasions of the Near East and Middle East. Goading some of the sharper graphic commentary has been the thriving of alternative weeklies and the movement of artists from the freebie press into Establishment dailies and syndicates. Even when cartoons have not explicitly attacked a sitting administration, they have reflected a cynicism about White House pronouncements that, at the very least, recalls the instinctive disenchantment of Mauldin's Willie and Joe.

More than occasionally, the cartooning treatment of the United States's foreign relations has come across as a war in everything but bullets. The need to lay out thorny international issues in the simplest and most direct terms possible has frequently found its solution in symbols—in national emblems (John Bull or the lion for Great Britain, the bear for Russia and the Soviet Union), in original icons (Herblock's Mr. Atom), and in situational representations (the turtle for the 1812 embargo, the swastika during World War II). The conflict inherent in diplomatic negotiations, let alone in open bilateral or multilateral discords, has been an invitation for cartoonists to indulge fight motifs, as a rule to a listlessly chauvinistic degree. A corollary effect has been the impression that every international issue is about winning and losing. Whatever a Henry Ladd Smith had to say, this was as much a thematic tradeoff for cartoonists back when James Madison was trying to stop the boarding of American ships at sea as it was when Harry Truman was distinguishing between leftists he found acceptable and ones he didn't.

The BLOODY MASSACRE perpetrated in King — Street BOSTON on March 5th 1770 by a party of the 29th REGT

Unhappy Boston! see thy Sons deplore,
Thy hallow'd Walks besmear'd with guiltless Gore.
While faithless P—n and his savage Bands,
With murd'rous Rancour stretch their bloody Hands;
Like fierce Barbarians grinning o'er their Prey,
Approve the Carnage, and enjoy the Day.

If scalding drops from Rage from Anguish Wrung
If speechless Sorrows lab'ring for a Tongue,
Or if a weeping World can ought appease
The plaintive Ghosts of Victims such as these;
The Patriot's copious Tears for each are shed,
A glorious Tribute which embalms the Dead.

But know Fate summons to that awful Goal,
Where Justice strips the Murd'rer of his Soul:
Should venal C—ts the scandal of the Land,
Snatch the relentless Villain from her Hand,
Keen Execrations on this Plate inscrib'd,
Shall reach a Judge who never can be brib'd.

The unhappy Sufferers were Mess.rs Saml Gray, Saml Maverick, Jams Caldwell, Crispus Attucks & Patk Carr
Killed. Six wounded: two of them (Christr Monk & John Clark) Mortally

Paul Revere's BOSTON MASSACRE (1770) triggered charges the
engraver had stolen the cartoon. *The Granger Collection, New York.*

When he wasn't concerned with Native Americans, Benjamin
Franklin turned his cartooning attentions to what Britannia
would look like without her American colonies (1767). *The
Granger Collection, New York.*

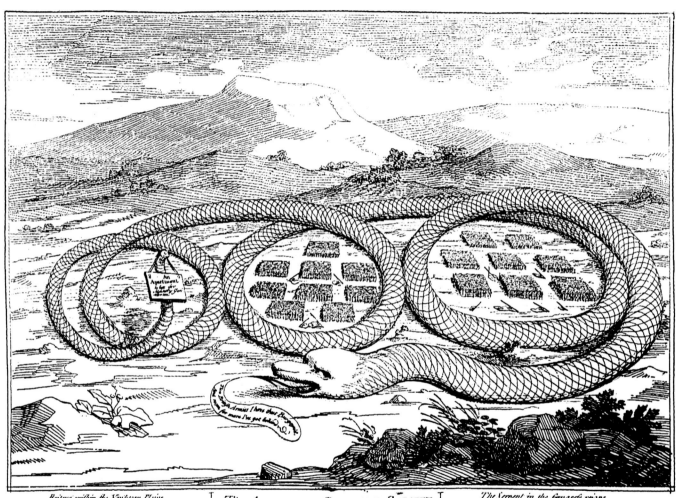

Britain's James Gillray acknowledged the victory of the colonists over England by using the snake symbol of Franklin's JOIN, OR DIE. *The Granger Collection, New York.*

BROTHER JONATHAN *Administering a Salutary Cordial to* JOHN BULL.

During the War of 1812, Amos Doolittle decided Brother
Jonathan needed to be rehabilitated as a national symbol (1813).
The Granger Collection, New York.

Charles's BATTLE OF LAKE ERIE (1813) jeered at the British in the aftermath of the Admiral Perry naval victory. *The Granger Collection, New York.*

Alexander Anderson's DEATH OF THE EMBARGO (1814) showed
President James Madison severing the head of the trade restrictions, as symbolized by a turtle. *The Granger Collection, New York.*

Adalbert Volck's view of the Civil War was that it was aimed at sacrificing the white man on an altar of "Negro worship" (1862). *The Granger Collection, New York.*

RECEPTION OF THE COPPERHEADS AT RICHMOND.

COPPERHEAD SPOKESMAN. "Be so kind as to announce to PRESIDENT DAVIS that a few of his Northern Friends wish to see him."

POMPEY. "De PRESIDENT desire me to say dat you is mistaken, Gemmen.   He haven't got no friends at de Norf; and when he wants any, he won't choose 'em among de *Peace Sneaks*."   (*Exeunt* COPPERHEADS *considerably abashed*.)—(*Vide* DAVIS's *Message*.)

Pro-Lincoln papers liked to think that not even Jefferson Davis would have been happy to see northern copperheads against the war (1863). *The Granger Collection, New York.*

Geography could be tapped as easily as religion and ethnicity ☞ for stereotyping, as witness the greeting accorded by President Andrew Johnson and Secretary of State William Seward to a representative from the newly purchased territory of Alaska. *The Granger Collection, New York.*

OUR NEW SENATORS.

Frank Bellew's IMPERIALISM CARTOON (1876) explicitly identified
the U.S. symbol as Jonathan although he wore Uncle Sam's
clothes. Jonathan and Russia's Ivan are shown reaching for Asia
by opposite routes. *The Granger Collection, New York.*

THE CUBAN MELODRAMA.

THE NOBLE HERO *(to the* HEAVY VILLAIN*).* — Stand back, there, gol darn ye! — If you force this thing to a fifth act, remember that's where I git in *my* work!

C. Jay Taylor's CUBAN MELODRAMA (1896) was of a piece with all the media propaganda about the island at the end of the nineteenth century—Uncle Sam as the dashing hero, Spain as the dastardly villain, and Cuba itself as a damsel in distress. *The Granger Collection, New York.*

UNCLE SAM'S NEW CLASS IN THE ART OF SELF-GOVERNMENT.

W. A. Rogers's Uncle Sam is the schoolteacher correcting Cuban revolutionary leader Maximo Gomez and Philippines insurgent Emilio Aguinaldo during the colonial wars at the end of the nineteenth century. *The Granger Collection, New York.*

CHRISTMAS IN OUR NEW POSSESSIONS.

SANTA CLAUS. — Phew! I 'm glad to oblige Uncle Sam, of course. But next time I come I 'll wear khaki!

An overheated Uncle Sam finds a Filipino child suspicious of his
Santa Claus disguise (1902). *The Granger Collection, New York.*

A BIGGER JOB THAN HE THOUGHT FOR.
UNCLE SAM—Behave, You Fool! Durn Me, If I Ain't Most Sorry I Undertook to Rescue You.

William Carson pictured a baffled Uncle Sam not understanding why Filipino leader Aguinaldo wasn't grateful for the U.S. takeover of his country. *The Granger Collection, New York.*

OPEN DOOR (1900) celebrates Uncle Sam's canniness in working out a trade pact with China while rivals England and Russia look on. *The Granger Collection, New York.*

HIS 128TH BIRTHDAY.

"Gee, but this is an awful stretch!"

Joseph Keppler, Jr.'s AMERICAN IMPERIALISM (1904) tallied up
the U.S. global presence from Puerto Rico to the Philippines.
The Granger Collection, New York.

Cabbages and Kings

"Army Medical Examiner: 'At last a perfect soldier!'"

Robert Minor's ARMY MEDICAL EXAMINER (1915) was exactly the kind of cartoon that led to the Wilson administration's crackdown on the socialist monthly *The Masses. The Granger Collection, New York.*

James Montgomery Flagg used himself as a model for the World
War I Uncle Sam poster of "I WANT YOU." *The Granger Collection,
New York.*

COMMITTEE ON PUBLIC INFORMATION

GEORGE CREEL, *Chairman*
THE SECRETARY OF STATE
THE SECRETARY OF WAR
THE SECRETARY OF THE NAVY

Bureau of Cartoons   *Bulletin No. 20*

BULLETIN FOR CARTOONISTS

OCTOBER 26, 1918

THE CARTOONIST MAKES PEOPLE SEE THINGS!

JAMES MONTGOMERY FLAGG

Flagg's cover for the government propaganda *Bulletin for Cartoonists* during World War I couldn't be accused of false modesty (1918). *The Granger Collection, New York.*

Boardman Robinson did not buy the Kaiser's 1915 claim that
"I . . . strove hard for peace even though war was inevitable."
The Granger Collection, New York.

Death was an inevitable figure in wartime cartoons, as in Louis Raemaekers's THE HARVEST IS RIPE (1916). *The Granger Collection, New York.*

THE SEAT OF TROUBLE

THE SEAT OF THE TROUBLE (1916) was typical of Luther Bradley's view of the warring forces in World War I. *The Granger Collection, New York.*

KULTUR HAS PASSED HERE (1916) was the kind of cartoon that brought charges against Raemaekers for jeopardizing Holland's neutrality during World War I and also reportedly made him an assassination target of the Germans. *The Granger Collection, New York.*

EDITOR   CAPITALIST   POLITICIAN   MINISTER

Having Their Fling

Art Young's HAVING THEIR FLING (1917) was the kind of anti-war
cartoon in *The Masses* that prompted the Wilson administration
to force the monthly out of business. *The Granger Collection,
New York.*

John McCutcheon campaigned futilely for the United States to join the League of Nations, warning congressmen that they would otherwise be planting the seeds for more wars. *The Granger Collection, New York.*

Clarence Batchelor's COME ON IN, I'LL TREAT YOU RIGHT. I USED TO KNOW YOUR DADDY (1936) won the Pulitzer Prize for 1937. *The Granger Collection, New York.*

Six months before the attack on Pearl Harbor, in June 1941, Charles Lindbergh and his pro-Hitler sentiments had already become Theodor Geisel's chief political target. *The Granger Collection, New York.*

Daniel Fitzpatrick published POLAND'S FALL (1939) only hours
before the Nazi invasion. *The Granger Collection, New York.*

Fresh, spirited American troops, flushed with victory, are bringing in thousands of hungry, ragged, battle-weary prisoners. (News item)

The cartoon for which Bill Mauldin was cited for his 1945
Pulitzer Prize. *The Granger Collection, New York.*

Even General Dwight D. Eisenhower concluded that running Mauldin's disenchanted GIs in *Stars and Stripes* was better for morale than suppressing them. *The Granger Collection, New York.*

Daniel Fitzpatrick's 1947 dialogue between Uncle Sam and the
Statue of Liberty ("Everybody is a little subversive but thee and
me, and sometimes I think even thee . . .") caught the red-
baiting paranoia in the United States in the post–WWII years.
The Granger Collection, New York.

L. J. Roche's FIRING OF MACARTHUR (1951) played to the tabloid sensibility of the time that President Truman, Secretary of State Dean Acheson, and the Pentagon were in the frying pan for removing Douglas MacArthur as the supreme commander in Korea after the general had gone public with his demands to bomb Chinese bases in Manchuria. *The Granger Collection, New York.*

Victor Weisz's OF COURSE I KNOW WHAT I'M DOING offered a chilling
look at the U.S. hydrogen bomb tests at Bikini in 1954. *The
Granger Collection, New York.*

The detonation of two atomic bombs in Japan in 1945 suggested to Fitzpatrick that the post–WWII world was faced with two contradictory questions. *The Granger Collection, New York.*

"It Looks Darling"

Mr. Atom was a regular Herblock character until, by the
cartoonist's admission, some readers found it "cute."
Copyright 1953 by Herblock in The Washington Post.

"HAVE A CARE, SIR"

THE SOUTH VIETNAMESE HAVE MADE GREAT PROGRESS. THEY ARE NOW BEARING THE BRUNT OF THE BATTLE. AND WE CAN NOW SEE THE DAY..

LET US END THE WAR. BUT LET US END IT IN SUCH A WAY THAT THE YOUNGER BROTHERS AND SONS OF THE BRAVE MEN WHO HAVE FOUGHT..

WHEN NO MORE AMERICANS WILL BE INVOLVED THERE AT ALL. AND THAT IS WHY I SAY TO YOU TONIGHT..

WILL NOT HAVE TO FIGHT AGAIN IN SOME OTHER VIETNAM AT SOME TIME IN THE FUTURE.

For Jules Feiffer, televised presidential speeches on Vietnam from Kennedy to Nixon amounted to lethal reruns. *Copyright Jules Feiffer, June 4, 1972.*

ᴈ⊐ Herblock's attacks on Joe McCarthy hardly spared Eisenhower for his lame responses to the Wisconsin senator's demagoguery. *From Herblock: A Cartoonist's Life (Times Books, 1998).*

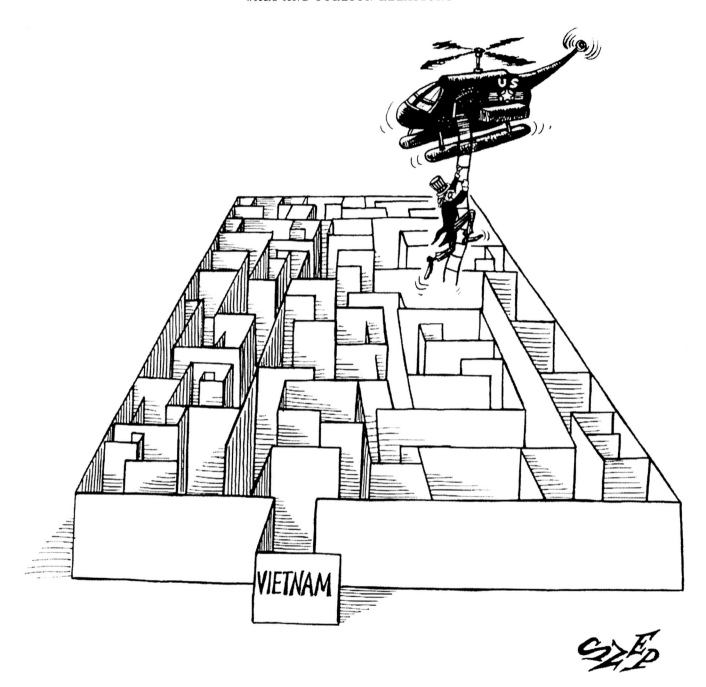

Richard Nixon sometimes took a back seat to Secretary of State Henry Kissinger when cartoonists like Jules Feiffer wanted to go after his administration's bloody connivance with dictatorships around the globe. *Copyright 1976 Jules Feiffer.*

Paul Szep's VIETNAM MAZE appeared years before the last U.S. personnel in Saigon actually were lifted out of the city by military helicopters. *Copyright 1973 Paul Szep/The Boston Globe.*

WHO LOST VIET NAM?

"NOT I," SAID IKE. "I JUST SENT MONEY."

"NOT I," SAID JACK. "I JUST SENT AD-VISORS."

"NOT I," SAID LYNDON. "I JUST FOLLOWED JACK."

"NOT I," SAID DICK. "I JUST HONORED JACK AND LYNDON'S COMMITMENTS."

"NOT I," SAID JERRY. "WHAT WAS THE QUESTION?"

"YOU LOST VIETNAM," SAID HENRY, "BECAUSE YOU DIDN'T TRUST YOUR LEADERS."

1·17·99 THE PHILADELPHIA INQUIRER. UNIVERSAL PRESS SYNDICATE.

Tony Auth's LIARS CLUB put the tawdriness of the Bill Clinton–Monica Lewinsky affair in the context of the far tawdrier military adventures of previous presidents. *Auth © 1999 The Philadelphia Inquirer. Reprinted with permission of Universal Press Syndicate. All rights reserved.*

Jules Feiffer's WHO LOST VIETNAM? was another variation on Nast's WHO'S TO BLAME? *Copyright 1973 Jules Feiffer.*

Jimmy Margulies reflected the tepid public support for the
Clinton administration's foray into Bosnia. *Copyright 1995 Jimmy
Margulies/The Record New Jersey.*

Mike Keefe found something a little odd about the Bush administration's steel position on stem cell research while simultaneously neglecting to provide necessary body armor for its troops in Iraq. © 2005 Mike Keefe/The Denver Post.

Ted Rall's BELIEVE ALL YOU CAN was one of the more searing cartoon takes on all the official lies told by the White House for justifying military escapades abroad. *Rall © 1998 Ted Rall. Reprinted with permission of Universal Press Syndicate. All rights reserved.*

Steve Benson's dim view of the purposes behind the latest ☞ invasion of Iraq. *Copyright 2003 Steve Benson/United Feature Syndicate. Reproduced by permission.*

IRAQ WAR
MEMORIAL

Robert Ariail's Jimmy Carter going off to monitor voting in
Florida anticipated similar cracks by the former president
himself in the wake of the 2000 electoral hanky-panky that led
to George W. Bush reaching the White House. *Copyright 2000
Robert Ariail/The State.*

3

Ethnic, Racial, and Religious Issues

Contentions that cartooning has played a significant role in American political events have a flip side. Indeed, a plausible argument could be made that editorial cartoons have historically had their single greatest impact in the dissemination of ethnic and racial stereotypes in the final decades of the nineteenth century. Caricaturing a Boss Tweed might have colored perceptions of Boss Tweed, maybe even of big city political bosses wherever they were to be found, but the grotesque figures of a Paddy or a Sambo as routine representations in a vast array of mainstream publications helped objectify existing biases toward an entire national or cultural group. That many of the publications carrying the cartoons were regarded as prestigious or were at the very least a part of everyday habits (qualities that couldn't be ascribed to such other period stereotype carriers as theatricals and minstrel shows) only made the objectification more "respectable" to those exposed to it. It was partly in this sense that Fischer noted that "the golden age of American political cartooning—the heyday of Nast, Keppler, and Gillam—was one in which ethical integrity warred against partisan and cultural hyperbole and lost, time and time again."[95]

If to considerably less shouting than motion pictures and television, cartooning's attempts in our day to romanticize ethnic groups, particularly through images of violence and sex, have produced the similar result not only of replacing one distortion with another but also of opening the door to political jabberwocky. Outraged that the mechanical use of such images as *The Godfather* and "The Sopranos" by cartoonists has left the implication that all Italians are *mafiosi*, for example, some protesting Italian-American organizations have gone to the ludicrous extreme of denying even the existence of a Mafia and insisting that Italian culture be identified exclusively with Michelangelo or Guglielmo Marconi. It has largely been thanks to such lopped posings of ethnic images—the African American depicted as a Guess-Who's-Coming-to-Dinner physician or a street hustler in the hood, the Chinese as a twelve-year-old genius in physics or the pimp-slaver of twelve-year-olds—that debates on so-called political correctness have ensued, creating yet another level of stereotypes. On slow days, cartoonists have had a choice between the suspect mind that has decreed the expression "Dutch treat" out of bounds for its offense to all people from the Netherlands and the merrily demented critics who have viewed such idiocies as the reason why civil rights legislation was never necessary for anybody (the choice for the journeyman cartoonist has usually been the former).

Ethnic and racial disparagements have seldom lacked a class component, to the point that poverty or bare-bones living has been depicted as the natural state of the group being ridiculed. This depiction has gone well be-yond any observation of immigrant realities. By and large, cartoonists have had little trouble accepting the premise that national background dictates economic status (negatively) when immigrating foreigners have been involved; on the other hand, when an imploded economy has affected generations-established ethnic groups, national background has become irrelevant. Thus during the Great Depression and its indifference to the surnames of the Johns and Marys lined up in front of soup kitchens, there was little attempt by cartoonists to particularize the scuffling masses: they weren't the Scots-Irish poor or the German-Dutch poor, they were just the vanilla poor known as "America."

As the late-nineteenth-century attacks on the Irish demonstrated, ethnic and religious caricatures were of-ten inseparable. But the identification of Irish Catholics with Democrats (later occasioned by Al Smith and John F. Kennedy) was hardly the only cartooning arena in-volving religion. Opposition to Jefferson—a constant of engravings around the turn of the nineteenth century—was fueled not a little by his deistic belief that all organ-ized religions were superfluous, and Federalist oppo-nents were quick to draft churchmen for charges that his election would lead to the confiscation of Bibles and the herding of wives and daughters to bordellos. As the evangelical *New England Palladium* put it in a warning against the Republican's reelection, "Should the Infidel Jefferson be elected to the Presidency, the seal of death is that moment set on our holy religion, our churches will be prostrated, and some infamous prostitute, under the title of the Goddess of Reason, will preside in the Sanctuaries now devoted to the Most High."[96]

There have also been precedents for the fundamen-talist Christian clouds that have hung over the George W. Bush administration and some of its domestic and international policy pronouncements. Perhaps most explicit of all—and most drawn by cartoonists—was McKinley in offering a rationalization for U.S. actions in the Philippines at the turn of the twentieth century. Interviewed by the *Christian Advocate*, he explained his decision to seize the archipelago by saying: "There was nothing left for us to do but to take them all [the islands], and to educate the Filipinos, and uplift and civilize and Christianize them, and by God's grace do the very best we could by them, as our fellow men for whom Christ also died."[97]

The chief pattern to the treatment of religion in the twentieth century was a reluctance to take on the organ-ized kind. With practically every daily in the country outside the *Wall Street Journal* vaunting itself as a "family paper," there was minimal enthusiasm for sponsoring cartoonists with skeptical views of mainline churches and their espoused Christian values. (Aside from the threat of tirades from the pulpit and picket lines outside the office, the social mixing of publishers and top edi-tors with prominent churchmen posed a problem.) Even dailies bent on blocking Smith's quest for the presi-dency in the 1920s for religious reasons found it more diplomatic to attack the Democrat for his opposition to Prohibition and other stances than for his Catholicism.

In Kennedy's case, the cover issue was how "soft" he was on godless communism.

The timidity did not extend to priests without formal backing from the Vatican or to preachers with radio station churches who decided their interpretation of Scripture entitled them to start satellite political groups for getting out the Word. One major figure of the kind was Father Charles Coughlin, whose pro-Nazi and anti-Semitic views in the 1930s aroused cartoonists from a general lassitude over developments in Germany. Later on, Jerry Falwell, Jim and Tammy Bakker, Jimmy Swaggart, Pat Robertson, and numerous other fundamentalists and evangelists clothing their right-wing politics in born-again Christianity became game, at least in northeastern cities where their influence wasn't especially strong. As with so many other topics, however, the restraints imposed by syndication made even cartoonists in the Northeast careful about alienating readers who believed Robertson's "700 Club" was a celestial talk show.

If there was any twentieth-century president whose religious background gave cartoonists an opening for ridicule, it was Carter. Particularly in the wake of lugubriously pedantic addresses to the nation on domestic economic problems, nobody was allowed to forget he was a Sunday School teacher. It was also during Carter's administration that mullahs and minarets began providing cartoonists with graphic shorthand for Near East and Middle East evil—a result most immediately of the fanatical rule of the Ayatollah Khomeini and the taking of American hostages in Iran. For the next twenty-five years, not least after the September 11, 2001, attacks on the Twin Towers and the Pentagon, Islamic images would play the threatening charge role Nast had once assigned to Catholic bishops and St. Peter's Basilica.

EUROPE

CHURCH & STATE

UNITED STATES.

A MILLERITE PREPARING FOR THE 23rd OF APRIL.
"Now let it come! I'm ready!!"

An 1843 lithograph mocks Adventist Church founder William Miller waiting for the Last Judgment within a well-stocked safe. Miller guessed wrong about the date for Armageddon more than once. *The Granger Collection, New York.*

21 Thomas Nast had a lot more confidence in European leaders than in American voters when it came to what he perceived as nefarious Vatican influences (1870). *The Granger Collection, New York.*

"I AM NOW INFALLIBLE."

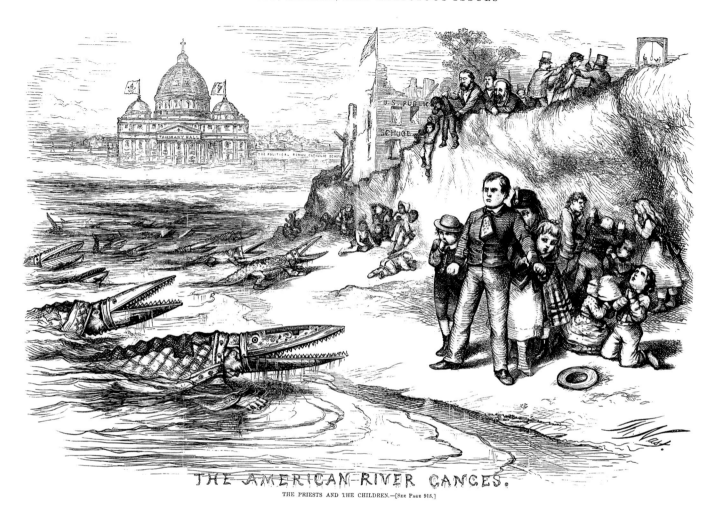

THE AMERICAN-RIVER GANGES.

THE PRIESTS AND THE CHILDREN.—[SEE PAGE 915.]

The artistic height of Nast's anti-Catholicism came with THE AMERICAN RIVER GANGES (1871), especially in the drawing of the crocodile heads as bishops' miters. *The Granger Collection, New York.*

Pius IX's declaration of papal infallibility in 1869 provided more grist for the Nast mill. *The Granger Collection, New York.*

THE RELIGIOUS VANITY FAIR.

Keppler's RELIGIOUS VANITY FAIR (1879) summed up his distaste for the various preachers and churches offering guarantees to salvation. At the same time, he wasn't beyond his own mawkishness, as in the trademark Puck advocating (*lower left*) "clean hands and a pure heart" as the ideal human course. *The Granger Collection, New York.*

Keppler never tired of twitting religious leaders, as in his so-called PHYSIOGNOMICAL STUDY of Pope Leo XIII in 1878. *The Granger Collection, New York.*

The "Pilgrim Fathers" of 250 Years Ago.
JUST AS DANGEROUS NOW AS THEN.
The "Pilgrim Fathers" of To-Day.

Frederick Burr Opper's 1883 cartoon suggested that arriving
immigrants were facing just as many perils as the Pilgrims had,
if of a different kind. *The Granger Collection, New York.*

FEBRUARY 7, 1885   COLUMBIA'S UNWELCOME GUESTS.

Frank Beard's COLUMBIA'S UNWELCOME GUESTS (1885) took the
anti-immigration line that an open-door policy could only lead
to an invasion by European anarchists, socialists, mafiosi, and
others perceived as sewer rats. *The Granger Collection, New York.*

C. Jay Taylor's INTERRUPTED IDYLL (1887) warned Mormon males that approaching antipolygamy laws were about to put an end to their leisurely supervision of toiling wives. *The Granger Collection, New York.*

AT FRISCO.

"See here, me Chinee Haythun, I'm wan of the Committee of National Safety; and bringing to me moind the words of George O'Washington and Dan'l O'Webster in regarrd to Furrin Inflooince, ye must go. D'ye understand? Ye must go!"

For Nast, there was only hypocrisy in any open arms by Irish immigrants to the Chinese that followed after them (1880).
The Granger Collection, New York.

THE EXTRA INDUCEMENTS OFFERED TO THOSE WHO WOULD GO WEST AT THE PRESENT TIME.

For Michael Angelo Woolf in the *Daily Graphic* (1874), Native Americans were the same as grasshoppers in the dangers they posed for settlers. *The Granger Collection, New York.*

ALARMING SYMPTOMS.

MRS. COHNSTEIN.— Lemline, I 'm afraid Ikey is sick.

MR. COHNSTEIN.— Vy, vat is der matter?

MRS. COHNSTEIN.— He lays in der gradle all day and don't dake no interest in anyding.

MR. COHNSTEIN.— Vat! don't dake no interest? Mine Gracious, he must be teadt!

Most anti-Semitic cartoons of the 1890s were lengthy dialogues laboring toward a punchline concerned with the money obsessions of Jews. *The Granger Collection, New York.*

BETWEEN TWO LOVES.

"Kin any one tell a po' culled man what to do in a case like dis?"

PUCK.

HE THAT
GIVETH TO THE
POOR LENDETH TO THE
LORD

OUR RELIGIOUS LANDLORDS AND THEIR ROOKERY TENANTS.

Taylor's OUR RELIGIOUS LANDLORDS AND THEIR ROOKERY TENANTS (1895) mocked the hypocrisy of New York landlords who found an hour for piety every Sunday in between week-long indifference to the misery of their slum tenants. *The Granger Collection, New York.*

☜ Sydney Griffin's BETWEEN TWO LOVES (1893) was a typically scabrous picture of the black man as being interested only in watermelon and chicken. *The Granger Collection, New York.*

OVERLOOKED—OR THE FOLLY OF FOREIGN MISSIONS.
Our church charities cannot see the misery under their own noses at home.

F. Victor Gillam was one of the many who detested the preoccupation of Christian missionaries with potential converts overseas while neglecting the hardships of people at home (1895). *The Granger Collection, New York.*

Marylanders didn't like it in 1931 when Edmund Duffy denounced the lynching of a black man by ridiculing their state song. *The Granger Collection, New York.*

"This is her first lynching."

Reginald Marsh's THIS IS HER FIRST LYNCHING (1934) broke with the usual cartooning fare to be found in *The New Yorker*. *The Granger Collection, New York.*

Theodor Geisel's WAITING FOR THE SIGNAL FROM HOME (1942) was published by *PM* literally hours before the order was given to intern Japanese Americans. *The Granger Collection, New York.*

Theodor Geisel's vision of U.S. employers using only the white keys was prompted by the 1942 White House ban on federal contracts to companies that practiced racial discrimination in job hiring during the war. *The Granger Collection, New York.*

Oliver Harrington's denunciations of the racism in American society ultimately forced him to live most of his life in Europe. One of his more noted pieces compared the school busing issue with the lynching of blacks. *Copyright 1972 Oliver Harrington.*

"THAT'S RIGHT— JIM AND TAMMY WERE EXPELLED FROM PARADISE AND LEFT ME IN CHARGE!"

A sex and fund misappropriation scandal that brought on the demise of TV preacher Jim Bakker and his wife Tammy Lee was no reason for celebrating, according to Doug Marlette, because it just afforded Jerry Falwell the opportunity to become even more sanctimonious. *Copyright 1987 Marlette/The Charlotte Observer.*

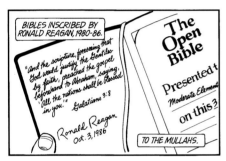

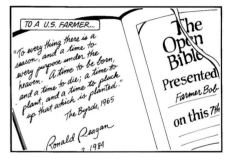

For Gary Trudeau, the Christian Right lobby behind Reagan provided one answer for all problems, both domestic and international. *Doonesbury © 1987 G. B. Trudeau. Reprinted with permission of Universal Press Syndicate. All rights reserved.*

According to Robert Ariail, a fundamentalist was fundamentally
a fundamentalist, whatever his specific religious fanaticism.
Copyright 2000 Robert Ariail/The State.

Nate Allen's sarcasm about the extent of pederasty among
Roman Catholic priests led to the loss of his job and a furor
in Michigan. *Copyright Nate Allen, The State News 2002.*

4

Local and Domestic Politics

By any practical standard, the *New York Times* had a more decisive impact than Nast on the demise of Boss Tweed. The paper's detailing of the extensive graft and fraud perpetrated by the Tammany Hall leader and his cohorts —information provided by a disaffected bookkeeper— animated a reformist faction within the Democratic Party and emboldened the criminal investigation that would ultimately land Tweed in prison. But Nast's art, especially in the cartoons that appeared in *Harper's Weekly* in the fall of 1871, has maintained a timeless power that history does not confer on daily newspaper stories, no matter how revelatory. In its own time, the relentless reduction of a supreme power broker to the seediest of carnival con men titillated in a way that the most elaborate tables of bribes and payoffs couldn't. Names and numbers didn't have banana noses.

The Nast series also defined the *editorial* in editorial cartooning—not mere graphic illustration of some statement of opinion on a masthead page, but an extension of reportorial disclosure (even, in this case, from another periodical). This journalistic function has little in common with the practice of publishers or editorial page directors to reduce the cartoonist's role to sheer visual reinforcement (or, in the case of the modern *Times* and other dailies, to not have one at all because of control issues). The paucity of memorable cartoons drawn within such a restriction since Nast's day has been a given for such artists as Oliphant, who has asked, "Does anyone really care any more whom [newspapers] endorse for President?"[98] As far back as 1866, some people were saying no, questioning the purpose of the prose editorials that routinely cued artwork. As writer-biographer James Parton put it in the *North American Review*,

The prestige of the editorial is gone. . . . [O]ur journalists already know that editorials neither make nor mar a daily paper, that they do not much influence the public mind, nor change many votes, and that the power and success of a newspaper depend wholly and absolutely upon its success in getting, and its skill in exhibiting, the news. . . .[99]

The cartoons with the greatest impact on local problems have been those linked most immediately to reportorial initiative rather than to some masthead declaration of principle. In their flamboyant visualizations, they haven't merely extrapolated from some politically or morally scandalous situation for synthetic commentary but have literally delineated practical threats to area inhabitants. If investigative reporters have been the cops bringing in the suspects, cartoonists have been the lineup for confirming the worst.

It has been in this local context that cartoonists have most earned medals as crusaders. However barbed, commentaries on national or foreign policy have rarely sustained practical force after being shot across the country to Washington. On the other hand, wardheelers, mayors, and governors have often shown impatience with newspapers that have insinuated they were less than luminous role models. When Nast and *Harper's Weekly* went after Tweed, they immediately heard knocks on the door. When Fitzpatrick and the *Post-Dispatch* had something to say about the "Rat Alley" sentences meted out to city racketeers in 1940, they were soon facing charges in the same St. Louis courtroom. In more than one case, the reprisals or attempted reprisals created the public attention the cartoons themselves might not have engendered.

The FEDERAL EDIFICE.
ELEVEN STARS, in quick fucceffion rife—
ELEVEN COLUMNS ftrike our wond'ring eyes,
Soon o'er the *whole*, fhall fwell the beauteous DOME,
COLUMBIA's boaft—and FREEDOM's hallow'd home.
  Here fhall the ARTS in glorious fplendour fhine !
And AGRICULTURE give her flores divine !
COMMERCE refin'd, difpenfe us more than gold,
And this new world, teach WISDOM to the old—
RELIGION here fhall fix her bleft abode,
Array'd in *mildnefs*, like its parent GOD !
JUSTICE and LAW, fhall endlefs PEACE maintain,
And *the* " SATURNIAN AGE," *return again.*

The Massachusetts *Centinel* celebrated the July 26, 1788, ratifica-
tion of the Constitution by New York with one of a series of
cartoons depicting the votes of the individual states as pillars
being erected. *The Granger Collection, New York.*

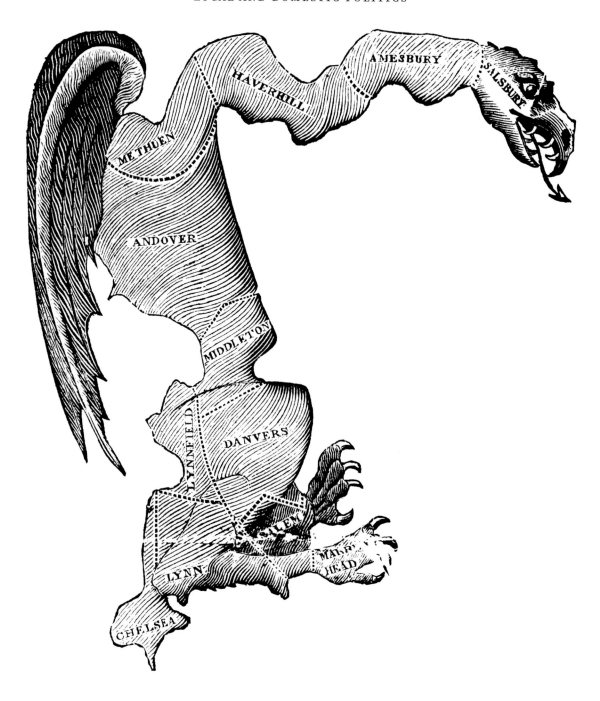

THE FORTY THIEVES OR THE COMMON SCOUNDRELS OF NEW-YORK.

Breaking up of a Grand Spree in the Tea Room & total abflustification of the common scoundrels.

Thomas Nast was hardly first in going after Tammany Hall, as evidenced by the 1840 lithograph THE FORTY THIEVES (OR, THE COMMON SCOUNDRELS OF NEW YORK). *The Granger Collection, New York.*

Elkanah Tisdale's 1812 creation of THE GERRYMANDER introduced a word into the English language. *The Granger Collection, New York.*

THE THIRD-TERM PANIC.

"An Ass, having put on the Lion's skin, roamed about in the Forest, and amused himself by frightening all the foolish Animals he met with in his wanderings."—SHAKSPEARE OR BACON.

Nast's Republican elephant made its first appearance in 1874 as a denial that Ulysses Grant was seeking a third term. *The Granger Collection, New York.*

A LIVE JACKASS KICKING A DEAD LION (1869) marked Nast's first ☞ use of the donkey as a symbol for Democrats. *The Granger Collection, New York.*

"A LIVE JACKASS KICKING A DEAD LION."

And such a Lion! and such a Jackass!

WHO STOLE THE PEOPLE'S MONEY? — 'TWAS HIM (1871) was a peak in
the Nast campaign against Tweed. *The Granger Collection, New York.*

A GROUP OF VULTURES WAITING FOR THE STORM TO "BLOW OVER."—"LET US *PREY*."

The power of Nast's cartoons against Tweed came not just from individual pieces but also from the relentlessness of the artwork in *Harper's Weekly*. *The Granger Collection, New York.*

[201]

"WHAT ARE YOU LAUGHING AT? TO THE VICTOR BELONG THE SPOILS."

THE TAMMANY TIGER LOOSE.—" What are you going to do about it?"

THE TAMMANY TIGER LOOSE (1871), Nast's powerful indictment of the Tweed ring, had more than one cartoon parent. *The Granger Collection, New York.*

Tweed himself was about the only survivor of the 1871 New York elections—leaving him to rule over a devastated kingdom. *The Granger Collection, New York.*

JEWELS AMONG SWINE.

"The police authorities, that do not enforce the laws against the liquor traffic, that do not suppress gambling or houses of ill repute......distinguished themselves on Saturday by arresting forty-three women, who went on the streets to sing and pray, and marching them to the station-house."—*Cincinnati Gazette.*

A COLD RECEPTION EVERYWHERE.

Joseph Keppler's Temperance Advocate in 1889 anticipated by decades Rollin Kirby's Mr. Dry. *The Granger Collection, New York.*

With JEWELS AMONG THE SWINE (1874), a denunciation of the Cincinnati police force's graft-ridden relationship with the liquor industry, Nast showed a concern for local politics beyond those of New York. *The Granger Collection, New York.*

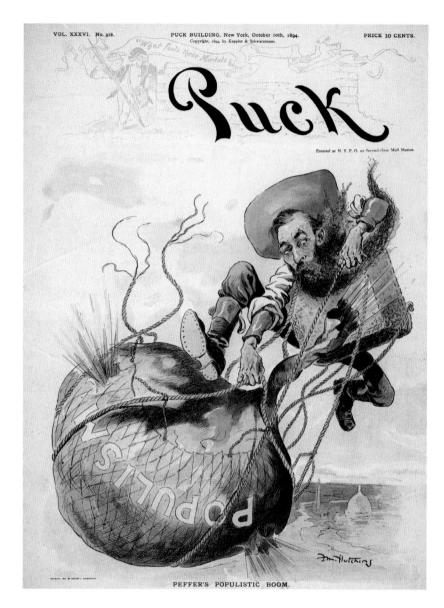

PEFFER'S POPULISTIC BOOM.

F. M. Hutchins was one of an army of *Puck* and *Judge* cartoonists
who wouldn't let William Alfred Peffer rest, in this case
depicting the Populist senator's balloon running out of air
over Washington. *The Granger Collection, New York.*

Laura Foster's MAKE WAY (1912) showed militant optimism about gaining women the vote. *The Granger Collection, New York.*

"Until Women Vote," by Rollin Kirby, from a 1915 issue of Woman's Journal.

Unlike most male cartoonists, Rollin Kirby suggested that woman's suffrage had an importance beyond itself in the pressures it would bring for ending the 72-hour work week and child labor (1915). *The Granger Collection, New York.*

"Your Honor, this woman gave birth to a naked child!"

For those not victimized by his fanatical moralistic crusades, Anthony Comstock was a figure of absurdity. In 1915, Robert Minor pictured him dragging a woman into court for having given birth to a naked child. *The Granger Collection, New York.*

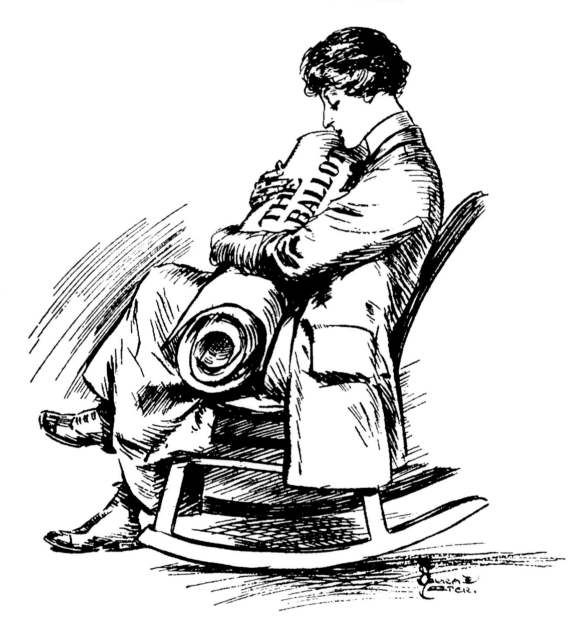

HUGGING A DELUSION

· LIFE ·

Bargain Day in Washington

Ellison Hoover's BARGAIN DAY IN WASHINGTON (1924) was one of the few effective cartoons on the Teapot Dome kind of corruption in the Harding administration that didn't depend on a tea kettle for its central image. *The Granger Collection, New York.*

Laura Foster's HUGGING A DELUSION (1915) caught her in a melancholy mood about the hopes for woman's suffrage. *The Granger Collection, New York.*

Rollin Kirby's Mr. Dry was inspired by a temperance figure
drawn by Joseph Keppler some four decades earlier (1920s).
The Granger Collection, New York.

"YOU DONE GOOD, SENATOR"

Rollin Kirby had little patience with "Cotton Tom" Heflin, an
Alabama senator who progressed through defenses of the
southern farmer to anti-Catholic tirades against Al Smith as a
presidential candidate to his blossoming as an unapologetic
white supremacist. YOU DONE GOOD, SENATOR was published in
1928. *The Granger Collection, New York.*

Daniel Fitzpatrick's ONE PERSON OUT OF EVERY TEN (1938)
conveyed the misery of the country during the Depression, when
10 percent of the population required public assistance for basic
survival. *The Granger Collection, New York.*

PAY DIRT

Daniel Fitzpatrick's PAY DIRT (1952) warned the Republicans
what they would come up with if they sought to benefit from Joe
McCarthy's red-baiting tactics. *The Granger Collection, New York.*

[215]

Jules Feiffer's Dancer was a familiar cartoon character during the turbulent 1960s. *Copyright Jules Feiffer Jan. 1, 1967.*

One of Jules Feiffer's favorite targets was middle-class hypocrisy on race questions. *Copyright 1963 Jules Feiffer.*

For Jimmy Margulies, the real political scandals that rocked New Jersey, many of them involving Italian Americans, ridiculed ethnic group protests against shows such as HBO's *Sopranos*. *Copyright 2001 Jimmy Margulies/The Record New Jersey.*

⌐⌐ I ME MINE MYSELF was Paul Conrad's epic sequel to *Ben Hur* during the Me Generation years. *Copyright 1978 Paul Conrad/Los Angeles Times.*

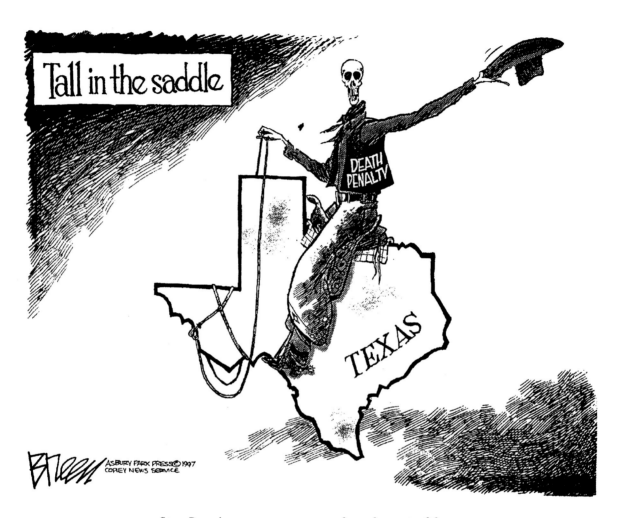

Steve Breen's TALL IN THE SADDLE made cowboy note of the
executions carried out regularly in President George W. Bush's
state. *Copyright 1997 Steve Breen/Asbury Park Press/Copley News Service.*

THE 9-11 HEARINGS...

For Steve Breen, the hearings into the intelligence failures of the White House, FBI, CIA, and other agencies prior to the 9/11 terrorist attacks ended up blaming everybody and nobody. *Copyright 2004 Steve Breen/San Diego Union-Tribune/Copley News Service.*

Ted Rall's skeptical look at some of the financial indemnities paid to those widowed by the Twin Towers attacks provoked personal demonstrations against the cartoonist. *Rall © 2004 Ted Rall. Reprinted with permission of Universal Press Syndicate. All rights reserved.*

Joel Pett was one of the first cartoonists to warn about the potential dangers of the Patriot Act. *Copyright 2003 Joel W. Pett, Lexington Herald-Leader. Reprinted with permission.*

Pat Oliphant's comparison of Attorney-General John Ashcroft to Mideast mullahs followed the passage of the Patriot Act. *Oliphant © 2001 Universal Press Syndicate. Reprinted with permission. All rights reserved.*

[5]

Business and Labor

Between the Civil War and World War I, few subjects entertained editorial artists more than the trusts. Pig-snouted, wolf-fanged, or bear-clawed, industrial greed was just about every animal in the menagerie that could leer from inside a brocaded vest. Fittingly, the monopoly figures were almost always outsized in comparison to other characters in a given tableau. Only slightly less stark over the years has been the treatment of banks, with their connotation of being where all the money is and maybe shouldn't be. Because they were usually so generic, the sallies against banks disturbed Establishment figures (including publishers of daily newspapers) only when presidents, most prominently Jackson and FDR, drafted laws for restricting their financial and monetary powers.

The trust and bank cartoons played into the folkloristic outlook that the real spirit of the country lay with the fabled "little guy" having to buck the power presumptions of Big Capital in everyday life. At the same time, however, there was almost always a baleful reaction when the little guy went beyond a victimistic concept of Labor to assert himself: Union with a capital "U" invited warnings to turn around. Even with the acceptance of unions in the twentieth century, there was far more cartoon emphasis in the mainstream press on their vulnerabilities (to communist infiltrators, racketeers, and corrupt leaders) than on the routine management abuses that had necessitated them in the first place. The prototype for this attitude was Keppler's disavowal of the need for a third political party when the radical economist Henry George stood as a Labor Party candidate in the 1886 New York City mayoralty race. The fact that George was popular enough to attract sixty-eight thousand votes and finish second ended up alarming Keppler rather than confirming his years-held outlook that voters wanted more choice than that between Republicans and Democrats.

WORKING MEN'S PARTY (1829) was a rare early example of a radical critique of election practices. While a millionaire conspires with the devil to buy an election, the average worker gives his vote to the ballot box. *The Granger Collection, New York.*

An 1837 lithograph pictures the consequences of the land specu-
lations and continuing friction between Washington and
banking interests that caused a depression. *The Granger Collection,
New York.*

THE MODERN COLOSSUS OF (RAIL) ROADS.

THE BOSSES OF THE SENATE.

Keppler's BOSSES OF THE SENATE (1889) was probably the most noted of the antitrust cartoons. *The Granger Collection, New York.*

꒱ Joseph Keppler's MODERN COLOSSUS OF (RAIL)ROADS (1879) was primarily directed at William Vanderbilt, but also squeezed in Cyrus Field (*left*) and Jay Gould (*right*). *The Granger Collection, New York.*

Frederick Burr Opper's 1885 solution for all the money problems attached to erecting the Statue of Liberty in New York harbor was to plaster the monument with advertisements. *The Granger Collection, New York.*

THE EMANCIPATOR OF LABOR AND THE HONEST WORKING-PEOPLE.—[SEE NEXT PAGE.]

Nast's 1874 anti-union piece THE EMANCIPATOR OF LABOR AND THE
HONEST WORKING PEOPLE made his views on organized labor
clear. *The Granger Collection, New York.*

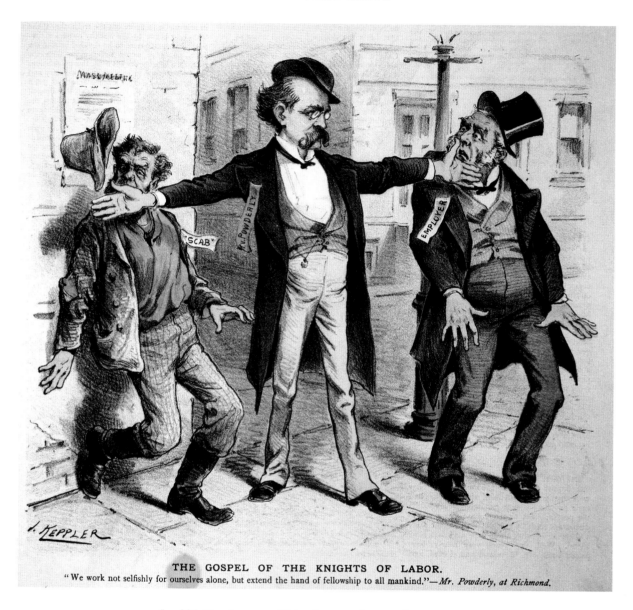

THE GOSPEL OF THE KNIGHTS OF LABOR.

"We work not selfishly for ourselves alone, but extend the hand of fellowship to all mankind."—*Mr. Powderly, at Richmond.*

In 1886, Keppler was sufficiently sympathetic to the unions to praise Knights of Labor leader Terence Powderly for giving the back of his hand to both a scab and an employer. *The Granger Collection, New York.*

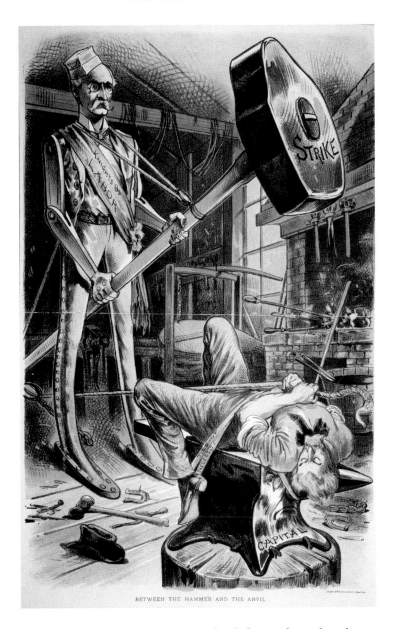

BETWEEN THE HAMMER AND THE ANVIL

Four years later, the same Keppler decided it was the worker who was caught between Powderly's hammer and Capital's anvil. *The Granger Collection, New York.*

THE GREAT AMERICAN COW (1896) attracted notoriety for being the
first cartoon entered into the *Congressional Record.* But although
the criticism of Wall Street's exploitation of western and
southern farmers gained its special fame from South Carolina
Senator Benjamin Tillman, it was actually drawn by Tom
Fleming of the New York *World. The Granger Collection, New York.*

A DISGUSTING AND SCANDALOUS CONDITION OF AFFAIRS.

COLUMBIA—Uncle Sam, How Long Are You Going to Sit Here Idle with that Nasty Mess in the National Door Yard? it is a Disgrace to the Nation and the People will not be Satisfied til there is a General Cleaning up. Even our European Neighbors are Disgusted and are Holding Their Noses. Stir Yourself and Get Rid of that Pile of Garbage Immediately!

The 1899 ARMY BEEF SCANDAL portrays Columbia urging Uncle Sam to do something about the tainted provisions being sent to troops in the Philippines. *The Granger Collection, New York.*

E

'S the Electric Trust.   Quick as a flash
He turns on his current and shocks out
your cash!

THE FREEDOM OF THE PRESS

Art Young's FREEDOM OF THE PRESS (1912) compared the news-paper world's hustling for advertising to the operations of a bordello. *The Granger Collection, New York.*

Opper's ALPHABET OF JOYOUS TRUSTS (1902) was the most ambitious attack on industrial monopolies. For the letter *E*, the cartoonist singled out the electricity industry. *The Granger Collection, New York.*

Rollin Kirby's TAIL HOLT (1929) predicted a ruinous bear market
three weeks before the Wall Street crash. *The Granger Collection,
New York.*

Gassing the Troops on Our Own Front Line

Theodor Geisel's GASSING THE TROOPS ON OUR OWN FRONT LINE
(1942) was a rare example of a mainstream cartoonist warning
that antilabor sentiments at home could compromise the U.S.
war effort. *The Granger Collection, New York.*

The Thinker

early Central American Free Trade Agreement

The Central American Free Trade Agreement (CAFTA)
promoted by the United States in the new millennium reminded
Kirk Anderson of earlier colonial transactions with Latin
America. *Copyright 2004 Kirk Anderson.*

Bud Shanks's Pulitzer Prize–winning THE THINKER was
typical of the cartoons that largely viewed labor unions
through the lens of corruption and radical infiltration.
Copyright 1957 Bruce Shanks/The Buffalo News.

Robert Ariail's succinct view of the manufacturing jobs leaving the United States for cheaper manpower. *Copyright 1993 Robert Ariail/The State.*

Notes

1. Stephen Hess and Milton Kaplan, *The Ungentlemanly Art: A History of American Political* Cartoons, (New York: Macmillan, 1975), 15.
2. Hess and Kaplan, 16.
3. Isabel Simeral Johnson, *Public Opinion Quarterly* 1 (July 1937): 37.
4. Kazimierz Michalowski, *Art of Ancient Egypt* (New York: Abrams, 1969), 82.
5. Hess and Kaplan, 51.
6. Roger Butterfield, *The American Past: A History of the United States from Concord to the Great Society* (New York: Simon and Schuster, 1966), 24.
7. Stephen Hess and Sandy Northrop, *Drawn and Quartered: The History of American Political Cartoons* (Montgomery, AL: Elliott & Clark Publishing, 1996), 36.
8. Hess and Northrop, 37.
9. Frank Luther Mott, *American Journalism: A History, 1690–1960* (New York: Macmillan, 1962), 400.
10. Cited by Hess and Kaplan, 41.
11. Richard Samuel West, *Satire on Stone: The Political Cartoons of Joseph Keppler* (Urbana: University of Illinois Press, 1988), 128.
12. *The Nation*, July 19, 1866, 408.
13. *The Nation*, April 11, 1872, 238.
14. Hess and Kaplan, 22.
15. Rollin Kirby, "My Creed as a Cartoonist," *Pep*, December 1918, 6.
16. Herb Block, *Herb Block's History: Political Cartoons from the Crash to the Millennium*, website, 1977 and 2000, 3.
17. Charles Press, *The Political Cartoon* (New York: Macmillan, 1981), 19.
18. Press, 243.
19. William Murrell, "Rise and Fall of Cartoon Symbols," *American Scholar* (Summer 1935): 306.
20. Butterfield, 51.
21. Fred Lewis Pattee, ed., *The Poems of Philip Freneau. Vol. I* (Princeton: Princeton University Library, 1902), 143.
22. Roger Fischer, *"Them Damned Pictures": Explorations in American Political Art* (New Haven, CT: Archon Books, 1996), 158.
23. Hess and Northrop, 28.
24. Roger Fischer, "Political Cartoon Symbols and the Divergence of Popular and Traditional Cultures in the United States," in *Dominant Symbols in Popular Culture*, ed. Ray B. Browne, Marshall W. Fishwick, and Kevin O. Browne (Bowling Green, OH: Bowling Green State University Popular Press, 1990), 205.
25. Hess and Kaplan, 1.
26. Mark W. Summers, *The Era of Good Stealings* (New York: Oxford University Press, 1993), 62.
27. Terry Ramsaye, *A Million and One Nights: A History of the Motion Picture through 1925* (New York: Touchstone [Simon & Schuster], 1926), 274.
28. *Punch*, July 15, 1843, 1.
29. Fischer, *Them Damned Pictures*, 46.
30. Butterfield, 262.
31. Fischer, *Them Damned Pictures*, 117.
32. *Harper's Weekly*, October 1879.

33. Herbert Mitgang, *The Fiery Trial: A Life of Lincoln* (New York: Viking, 1974), 149.

34. Albert Bigelow Paine, *Thomas Nast: His Period and His Pictures* (New York: Harper and Brothers, 1904), 129.

35. Arthur Bartlett Maurice and Frederic T. Cooper, *The History of the Nineteenth Century in Caricature* (New York: Dodd, Mead, 1904), 233.

36. Harry Thruston Peck, "Here and There," *Bookman*, October 1900, 117.

37. Hess and Kaplan, 127.

38. Hess and Kaplan, 126.

39. Philadelphia *North American*, January 27, 1903, 1.

40. Philadelphia *North American*, January 30, 1903, 1.

41. Philadelphia *North American*, May 18, 1903, 6.

42. Allan Nevins and Henry Steele Commager, *The Pocket History of the United States* (New York: Pocket Books, 1942), 270.

43. *The Arena*, April 1905, 70.

44. Fischer, "Political Cartoon Symbols and the Divergence of Popular and Traditional Cultures in the United States," 205.

45. New York *Record*, March 5, 1896, 1.

46. Elizabeth Knowles, ed., *The Oxford Dictionary of Quotations* (Oxford: Oxford University Press, 1999), 367.

47. Hess and Northrop, 72.

48. *The Christian Advocate*, January 22, 1903, 1.

49. Hess and Kaplan, 141.

50. Richard Fitzgerald, *Art and Politics* (Westport, CT: Greenwood Press, 1973), 13.

51. Lloyd Goodrich, *John Sloan* (New York: Macmillan, 1952), 41.

52. John T. McCutcheon, *Drawn from Memory* (Indianapolis, IN: Bobbs-Merrill, 1950), 199.

53. Jan Cohn, *Creating America: George Horace Lorimer and the Saturday Evening Post* (Pittsburgh, PA: University of Pittsburgh Press, 1989), 1.

54. James G. Harbord, president of the Radio Corporation of America, cited by *The Review of Reviews*, April 1929, 89.

55. Art Young, *Art Young: His Life and Times* (New York: Sheridan House, 1939), 427.

56. Hess and Northrop, 100.

57. "Mauldin at War, 1943–1945," *Bill Mauldin beyond Willie and Joe*, an online tribute from the collections of the Library of Congress, August 7, 2003.

58. Allan Nevins and Frank Weitenkampf, *A Century of Political Cartoons: Caricature in the United States from 1800 to 1900* (New York: Scribner's, 1944), 134.

59. Werner Hofmann, *Caricatures from Leonardo to Picasso* (New York: Crown, 1957), 54.

60. *American Scholar* (Autumn 1936): 472.

61. Henry Ladd Smith, "The Rise and Fall of the Political Cartoon," *Saturday Review*, May 29, 1954, 7.

62. Walt McDougall, *This Is the Life* (New York: Knopf, 1926), 219.

63. Press, 198.

64. Quoted by Lee Judge in "Why Political Cartoonists Sell Out," *Washington Monthly*, September 1988, 38.

65. Judge, 39.

66. Bill Mauldin, *Back Home* (New York: William Sloane Associates, 1947), 263.

67. Fischer, *Them Damned Pictures*, 222.

68. Doug Marlette, "Journalism's Wild Man," *American Journalism Review*, January–February 1992, 32.

69. Quoted in "Quintessential Cartooning: The Political Art of Pat Oliphant," *Target*, Summer 1982, 8.

70. William Murrell, *A History of American Graphic Humor*. Vol. 2 (New York: Cooper Square Publishers, 1967), 263.

71. Los Angeles *Times*, March 18, 1973, part 6, 5.

72. Mrs. Walt Kelly and Bill Crouch, Jr., eds., *The Best of Pogo* (New York: Simon and Schuster, 1982), 224.

73. Press, 334.

74. Press, 369.

75. Gary Groth, *Drawing the Line* (Seattle, WA: Fantagraphic Books, 2004), 37.

76. WashingtonPost.com, November 18, 2004.

77. *Wall Street Journal*, April 16, 1984, 32.

78. Chris Lamb, *Drawn to Extremes: The Use and Abuse of Editorial Cartoons* (New York: Columbia University Press, 2004), 113.

79. Hess and Northrop, 152.

80. Lamb, 206.

81. *Newsweek*, October 13, 1980, 77.

82. Hess and Northrop, 128.

83. Block, 2.

84. Ed Stein, "Squeezing Originality out of Editorial Cartoons," *Nieman Reports*, Winter 2004, 38.

85. Hess and Kaplan, 33.

86. Bill Watterson, "The Cartoonist's License," *Target*, Winter 1982, 18.

87. Lamb, 145.

88. J. P. Trostle, "Do We Still Matter?," Association of American Editorial Cartoonists website, September 2002.

89. Richard H. Minear, *Dr. Seuss Goes to War: The World War II Cartoons of Theodor Seuss Geisel* (New York: New Press, 1999), 7.

90. Statement confirmed and reiterated to the author, June 14, 2005.

91. *New York Times*, June 13, 2005, C1.

92. Hess and Northrop, 130.

93. Hess and Kaplan, 116.

94. *Cosmopolitan*, December 1951, 35.

95. Fischer, *Them Damned Pictures*, 12.

96. *New England Palladium*, September 7, 1802, 1.

97. *Christian Advocate*, 1.

98. Pat Oliphant, "Why Political Cartoons Are Losing Their Influence," *Nieman Reports*, Winter 2004, 25.

99. *North American Review*, April 1866, 375.

Index

About the Author

Donald Dewey has published twenty-five books of fiction, nonfiction, and drama. His awards include the Nelson Algren Prize for Fiction. His biographies of actors James Stewart and Marcello Mastroianni have been hailed in both the United States and Europe. His history of baseball fans, *The Tenth Man*, was cited by numerous publications as one of the best books of 2004, as was his biography (written with Nicholas Acocella) of Hal Chase, *The Black Prince*. In both his books and in hundreds of magazine articles, Dewey has written extensively of late-nineteenth-century American history—a key period for the present study of U.S. cartooning.

✍

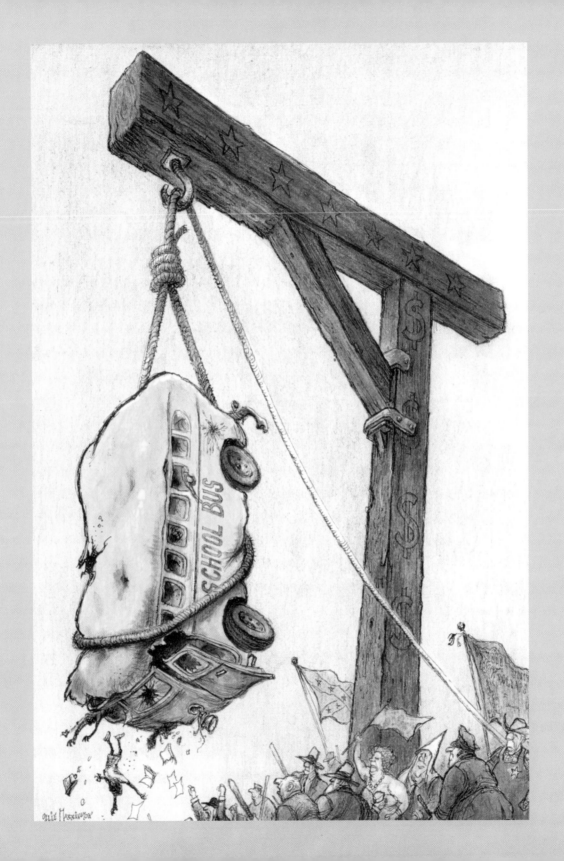